The Rain At the End of the Summer

John B. Keane

The Rain At the End of the Summer

MERCIER PRESS
IRISH PUBLISHER – IRISH STORY

MERCIER PRESS

Cork
www.mercierpress.ie

First published in 1968 by Progress House (Publications) Ltd.
This edition 2015

© John B. Keane Occasions, 1967

ISBN: 978 1 78117 480 7

The Rain at the End of the Summer is a copyright play and may not be performed without a licence. Application for a licence for amateur performances must be made in advance to the Drama League of Ireland, The Mill Theatre, Dundrum, Dublin 16. Terms for professional performances may be had from JBK Occasions, 37 William Street, Listowel, Co. Kerry.

This book is sold subject to the condition that it shall not, by way of trade or otherwise, be lent, resold, hired out or otherwise circulated without the publisher's prior consent in any form of binding or cover other than that in which it is published and without a similar condition including this condition being imposed on the subsequent purchaser.

No part of this publication may be reproduced or transmitted in any form or by any means, electronic or mechanical, including photocopying, recording or any information or retrieval system, without the prior permission of the publisher in writing.

All characters, locations and events in this book are entirely fictional. Any resemblance to any person, living or dead, which may occur inadvertently, is completely unintentional.

Printed and bound in the EU.

To Michael Twomey of Cork

'THE RAIN AT THE END OF THE SUMMER' was first produced by The Southern Theatre Group at the Gaiety Theatre, Dublin on Monday, June 19th, 1967. The cast was as follows:-

Joss O'Brien	JAMES N. HEALY
Toddy O'Brien	DERMOT CROWLEY
Ellie O'Brien	EILISH McSWEENEY
Jamesy O'Brien	JIM NORTON
Kate	MAIRIN MORRISH
Penny	ABBEY SCOTT

Production by Dan Donovan
Scenery by Frank Sanquest

ACT ONE

SCENE 1

[A blisteringly hot summer's day.
THE TIME is the present
The family of JOSS O'BRIEN have just finished lunch in the back-garden of their home.
JOSS is a plump, aged, prosperous widower, retired from a business in the city.
TODDY, his eldest son is stretched full-length on the grass, eating ice-cream from a saucer.
JOSS, himself, is relaxed at the head of the table, idly scanning a newspaper.
JAMESY, his second son, is smoking at the table, looking into space.
ELLIE, his daughter, youngest of the family, is examining the shrubbery near the back wall]

Joss [*Reading aloud*] "Five drowning fatalities in a week!" Too many! Far too many! Five, imagine! Five people. Five families deprived of people they genuinely love.

Toddy People *will* swim alone. You can put it down to ignorance.

Joss Or to bravado.

Ellie It's sad. It really is.

Jamesy You can put it down to overconfidence.

Joss You can really put it down to this wonderful weather. Very few people drown when it's frosty.

Ellie There's a nest here!

Toddy A bird's nest?

Ellie It looks like a bird's nest.

Toddy Don't touch it and don't breathe into it.

Ellie Why not?

Toddy You'll evict the tenant. If you breathe into a bird's nest, the birds leave it.

Ellie Really? I didn't know!

Joss Has it got any eggs in it?

Ellie NO! It's empty.

Toddy Probably hatched and fledged under our noses. Imagine that! A whole family broken up in a single season.

Joss I used to search for birds' nests when I was a boy. You had to wait till June, of course, when the branches were well outfitted with leaves, when there were secret pockets where the birds could hide their eggs. There weren't any cinemas or television sets in those days. It was an older boy who got us into the habit…

Eugie O'Leary...Monsignor Eugie O'Leary now in Los Angeles, St. Mary of the Angels in San Lavinia Valley. You remember him, Toddy? You met him in Crosshaven the summer after Mammy passed away.

Toddy Oh, yes! Monsignor O'Leary! He taught me how to swim.

Joss As I say, we spent our days hunting for nests, and fishing—fly-fishing for brown trout. Jamesy, you were barely able to walk then. I often half-murdered you until I found out you didn't like fishing. But you forgave me, Jamesy...I thought you never would. *[Jamesy is absorbed with his thoughts]* And I can tell you all the hour and the minute that Jamesy forgave me. Do you remember, Jamesy?...Jamesy!

Jamesy Yes, Dad!

Joss It was the day I took him to Limerick when Munster drew with Australia in the snow. What a match that was? And what a bigoted referee? Munster should have walked it. God, I felt indignant when he disallowed that try, and Jamesy...*[Laughs]* he was nine then...wanted to leap the barrier.

[Jamesy laughs obediently, not disrespectfully. He broods]

Joss But about birds' nests. One summer when I was ten...or was it eleven, I'm not sure now...anyhow I found twenty-seven. You wouldn't find them now.

The countryside is being eaten up...I'll bet if you went out today...

Ellie   Dad!

Joss   Yes, Ellie.

Ellie   I hate to butt in, but...

Joss   *[Fondly]* What is it?

Ellie   How long more do we eat out here?

Joss   For as long as the fine weather lasts, Ellie. We must make the most of the fine days ...Why? Don't you like it?

Ellie   I like it. I love it, but didn't Toddy tell you?

[Toddy, laughingly leaps from his position and smothers Ellie's mouth with his hand. Ellie manages to speak].

Ellie   Penny is coming. His beautiful, bonny Penny is coming for her first week-end.

Toddy   *[Releases her]* I was waiting for the right moment Dad, but trust blabbermouth here to pip me.

Joss   But that's marvellous, Toddy! When?

Toddy   She said she'd like to come this week-end. Anyway, I need your O.K.

Joss   My O.K.? Good God, man, I'm touched that

in this day and age a man who can support himself should ask such a question.

Toddy Eh?…What question?

Joss That you should ask for permission to bring your girl for a week-end. Most fellows of your age would take it for granted. I'm delighted, Toddy. Delighted she's honouring us with her company.

Ellie Now, can I talk - now that it's a surprise no longer?… She's one of the Cassidy's from Donnerry…*[Dodges Toddy]* …She's not like the rest of the Cassidys, though. This one is pretty.

Joss I've heard of the Cassidys. They're a very old family, Toddy, and a highly respected one. There was a Cassidy in Donnerry in the reign of Elizabeth the First. There was a Finian Cassidy an Archbishop of Cashel. There was a General Thomas Cassidy…

Ellie *[She sits on Joss's lap]* Dad…eating out-of-doors in Ireland…it's unheard of.

Joss It's the weather.

Ellie Seriously, Dad, what will she think?

Toddy I was going to say the same thing, but I thought it disrespectful…But does it matter?

Joss I see! And what have you got to say, Jamesy?

Ellie   He's in a very thoughtful mood today.

Joss   No, he isn't! I would say he's a man with a problem. Anything the matter, Jamesy?

Jamesy   No, Dad…no!

Joss   Anything wrong in the shop? Want me to come in?

Jamesy   No need, Dad. The shop is fine. It's probably the heat. I find it a bit depressing. A good swim is what I need.

Joss   You all know why he's called Jamesy?

ALL   Yes…yes…*[Laughing]* …We all do.

Joss   Your mother's father, oul' Jamesy Pain. I'll never forget the day I told him I wanted his daughter's hand.

Ellie   We know, Dad…And now, before you go back any further where were we?

Joss   Oh, yes! The question of eating out here. *[Eases Ellie upwards and rises].* It's always nice to see young people concerned. But for whom are they concerned, that's the question.

Toddy   For you, Dad, of course. I don't care and I know Penny won't.

Ellie   I'll eat out here in a blizzard…I hope we get a

blizzard to show how much we all care for you.

Joss That's very nice of you, Ellie, and just for that we'll eat indoors. Majority should rule and if you feel that this girl might be discomfited, I vote we move in right away.

Ellie We'll do nothing of the kind. We were thoughtless.

Toddy For as long as the weather holds fine, we'll eat out here. All agreed? I know she'll love it.

Joss Whatever you want… *(Goes to where Jamesy is sitting)*. What's wrong with my co-Director today?

[Jamesy smiles affectionately and, over his shoulder, takes his father's hand].

Jamesy Nothing in the world, Dad.

Joss Probably the heavy summer. *[Moves away]* You remember Keats' poem about the Autumn and the Bees: *"Until they think warm days will never cease for summer has overbrimmed their clammy cells …"* and there was another poem - the only other one I remember - *"All along the backwater, through the rushes tall, ducks are a-dabbling, up tails all, ducks tails, drakes' tails, yellow feet a-quiver, yellow feet all out of sight, a-busy on the river"*.

Toddy There are better poems, but that one has something.

Joss I learned it by heart off my own bat when I was seven…Isn't anybody going to go to work today?

[Enter the housekeeper, Kate].

Kate Ten minutes to two! All the other people in the city are going back to work.

Ellie Trust Kate! Now why in heaven don't you marry Kate, Daddy? Put on a bikini, Kate, and seduce him.

Joss Great idea!

Ellie Housekeeper for nine years and not a breath of scandal.

Toddy Well, he must be abiding by the rules. We'd have heard something at some stage.

[Kate playfully dodges them and considers ware on table]

Kate I overheard the bit about Toddy's girl. I think we'll be able to cater for her all right. *[To Joss]* But, don't forget, you're taking me to Blane on Sunday,

Joss Yes, Blane. We can't forget Blane.

ALL *[Echo]* Blane!

Ellie If Kate didn't go to Blane, she'd die. What is it about Blane, Kate?

Jamesy The corn and old-fashioned country people and the secret shining streams.

Toddy Blane of the surging sea-trout, the golden corn..

Ellie Blane of the partridges and pleasant old-fashioned ways.

Kate Blane is my home!

Toddy Nobody knows better than I do how pleasant it is. When I was fractious and childish you took me there, Kate, and grounded me solid into the honest ways of the countryside. Your brother is married now, Kate, isn't he?

Kate It's still my home. I like to visit it now and again.

Joss Don't worry! I'll see you get there on Sunday.

Toddy To work, children!

Joss Look at them! Toddy, Solicitor, eager and bright and just; Ellie, Secretary in the most important industry in our fair city, and Jamesy…well all I can say about Jamesy is that business has doubled since I retired… what more can I say? The evidence is overwhelming and every particle of it in favour of this family. We had our ups and downs. I won't go into my drinking days. Nightmares of alcoholism. But we won, thanks to yourselves and Kate. I conquered it and it wasn't easy. Looking at all of you it was worth it.

Ellie I think a bow is in order.

[Toddy and Ellie bow. Jamesy bows belatedly].

Toddy *[To Jamesy]* Coming with us?

Jamesy No! You go ahead. I have to make a few phone calls. They don't know in the shop whether I'm coming back for the rest of the day or not, and that's the way I want it.

Joss Isn't that unfair? I always arrived on the dot the same as every man, woman and child who worked for me. It seems unfair!

Jamesy No! Keep them guessing! Anyhow, these are very personal calls. McLaverty's have a job lot worth seventeen hundred. I think it can be bought for fifteen hundred. Hard cash, of course,

Joss You're the boss!

Toddy O.K.! See you at supper, Dad.

[Ellie kisses her father goodbye. Joss stays seated. Toddy and Ellie give brief farewells to Jamesy and Kate. Exit Toddy, preceded by Ellie].

Joss *[To Kate, who is re-arranging table]* A lovely meal,

Kate Wasn't it, Jamesy?

Jamesy Always is! No bother to Kate.

Kate The meal is no good if the appetite isn't there in the first place.

Jamesy I'd better make those calls. Excuse me. *[He is about to exit]* By the way, Dad, you're not going anywhere, are you?

Joss Why, no Jamesy, no. Is there something you want to discuss?

Jamesy Yes, there is, but I'll make the calls first. Just so long as I know where to find you…

[Exit Jamesy. Joss immediately puts his hand around Kate]

Kate Careful! What if Jamesy should come back?

Joss He's making a phone call, isn't he? Come on! Just one quick kiss.*[They kiss swiftly]* I wonder what she's like…Toddy's girl, I mean?

Kate She comes from a very respectable family.

Joss Yes, I know. We mightn't be as old a family but I think we're respectable.

Kate Self-praise is no praise!

Joss Oh, I didn't say it. I remember, after her death, when I was on the booze, I heard a woman say in the shop one day…. "Isn't it a shame to see such a respectable man drinking?" So, you see, others think me respectable. Although I really sunk to indescribable depths when I was hitting the bottle. Nobody knows but yourself and myself. I'm sure she's a nice person.

Kate I've never seen the girl, but Toddy's nobody's fool. If she likes Toddy, she's bound to be nice.

Joss Well, we'll soon find out. Funny, isn't it? Yesterday they were kids and today…well, it's quite a change. Time has a nasty habit of creeping up behind a man, unawares. I've been thinking a good deal lately, Kate. I suppose it's because I've got nothing else to do. I should have stayed with the business, but then, Jamesy deserved his chance. Thinking becomes a habit…you might say, an obsession. Anyway, the gist of it is, I've decided to tell them about us.

Kate You mustn't!

Joss But, Goddammit, we cannot go on like this; it's ridiculous and if they won't understand now, they'll never understand.

Kate No…you can't, Joss…they mightn't approve. You don't know what kids are like.

Joss You want to go on like this for ever, then? Is that it?

Kate No, you know that isn't true, but we could wait a while…a little while.

Joss Until all three are married. Is that what you mean?

Kate It might be wiser.

Joss   Well, Goddammit, I won't! I won't waste any more time. I'm getting old, Kate. In eight years I'll be seventy…and you're not getting any younger.

Kate   Wait until after Toddy's married, at least. We could prepare them in easy stages.

Joss   But you heard what Ellie said a moment ago. She asked why I didn't propose to you.

Kate   *[Laughs]* A joke, Joss. That was a joke. Ellie might not see the joke any longer if it were true. I just can't see Toddy smiling when you tell him, or Jamesy either. They take me for granted. They'll never see me as anything but Kate, Kate the house-keeper…but to have to accept me as a mother, Oh, God, no! They'll never do that.

Joss   I've thought about my children long enough. No father could have done more than I did. It's time I thought about myself. They owe it to me and they owe it to you. You've cared for them over nine years. You've been a second mother to them.

Kate   I know that. *[Laughs bitterly]* But it's the first mother they remember and that's only right and natural.

Joss   I'll tell you what I really think…

Kate   What?

Joss   I think we're taking too serious a view of it. I think they'll be delighted when we tell them.

Kate Maybe. Maybe not. I think not.

Joss They ought to be delighted, and I think they will. Goddammit, I've waited nine years. At my age, that's the best part of a lifetime. What do you want…an impotent old man with a leg in the grave?

Kate You're a nice one, to talk like that!

[He seizes her playfully but she avoids him and gathers a handful of ware from the table]

Kate I've got work to do, lover! Out of my way. We're going to Blane, Sunday?

Joss Oh, God, yes! The sky would fall, wouldn't it, if we didn't go to Blane? But let's go early and have lunch at Crosshaven on the way. The kids can get their own.

Kate Are you mad? 'Twould be the talk of the city the day after.

Joss But I take you to Blane every Sunday and there's never any talk.

Kate Blane is where I was born and there's nothing wrong about that. Besides, you've the name of being a good employer. It's only what people would expect from you, to take your servant to her home on Sunday. It's natural, like driving a person to Mass.

Joss Don't say servant!

Kate Well, it's what I am.

Joss You're my housekeeper.

Kate And when a man marries his housekeeper, what happens?

Joss Everybody accepts it.

Kate No! The dirt in people's minds comes to the surface.

Joss You're worrying about nothing! People just joke about these things.

Kate I agree with you…*[Pause]* …The bother is that it's always a dirty joke.

[Exit Kate, with arms full of crockery. Joss shakes his head, takes his paper, folds it neatly, thrusts it behind a creeper on the back wall and is about to go into the house when Jamesy enters. They almost collide].

Jamesy Oh!…Are you going somewhere?

Joss No…nowhere…Come on, sit down.

[Joss seats Jamesy and returns to his own seat at head of table. He smothers a laugh].

Jamesy Something funny?

Joss Yes, I suppose you could call it funny. Just something that occurred to me.

Jamesy Oh!

Joss *[Elaborately explanatory]* I see myself here and now at this moment and my mind goes back. Back to your grandfather, oul' Jamesy Pain. The day of your christening, we were sitting here—right here where we are now. We were celebrating. We were tight—tight as two new drums. He got up to go to the toilet. "This is damn funny", he said. "What's funny?" I asked him. "Well," he said, "here I eat in the back garden and if I want to go to the lavatory I have to go into the house. At home I eat in the house and if I want to go to the lavatory I go out to the backgarden". He was a gay man, oul' Jamesy. *[Both laugh]* …You wanted to see me about something?

Jamesy Yes, but I don't know how to begin. It's an awkward business and my only worry is, how're you going to take it.

Joss Well, then, the only cure is to spit it out. I may have a little more understanding than you'd give me credit for.

Jamesy *[Irritated with himself]* I don't know. I don't know, Dad…I don't know how to begin. It's difficult.

Joss All right. I'll help you. Now, let's see. Is somebody fiddling in the shop?

Jamesy No! That's all sewn up since I installed the new system.

Joss You've given too much credit.

Jamesy No.

Joss Ah, I've got it…you're getting married!

Jamesy It's not as simple as that, Dad.

Joss You're afraid I'll hit the whiskey-bottle again.

Jamesy That never even occurred to me. *[Aside]* Not yet anyway.

Joss Well, what is it, son? If you can't tell me now right away, don't try too hard. It will come out by itself. Or maybe you'd like to think about it for a while longer and tell me over a few drinks tonight. Is it bad, Jamesy?

Jamesy I don't know. It all depends on how you look at it.

Joss Is it me? Is it something I've done or something you might think I'm likely to do?

Jamesy No.

Joss Thank God for that. I've got my worries, too, you know. Now, don't you think you'd better tell me. You won't get a more sympathetic hearing anywhere.

Jamesy   I want to, Dad, but now that I've the opportunity I can't.

Joss   Look, Jamesy, we'll have a few drinks tonight and you can tell me then. It's always easy over a drink. O.K.?

Jamesy   O.K., Dad! I'll see you tonight.

Joss   Don't look so down and out. *[Puts his hand on Jamesy's shoulder as Jamesy is about to depart]* Whatever it is, we're in it together. Remember that.

Jamesy   Yes, Dad.

Joss   And you'll find, Jamesy, as I often did, that it will be all the same in a very short time. Everything passes.

Jamesy   I hope so. See you tonight then but be prepared for a bit of a shock.

[Exit Jamesy]

Joss   *[Half to himself]* A shock! A bit of a shock!

[Joss is perplexed and a little worried when Kate enters]

Kate   What was all that about?

Joss   Don't know! He didn't tell me and I didn't press him. He promised to tell me tonight over a drink.

Kate   He looks worried. You know he hasn't been sleeping lately?

Joss No, I didn't know.

Kate I've heard him moving around at all hours.

Joss It might be that he's in love.

Kate If he is, it's not making him very happy. *[She busies herself at the table]* I don't think it's love.

Joss Maybe he's overstocked, or his overdraft's out of hand...but it couldn't be that. I'd know if it were. *[Moves towards exit]* Something's wrong! I feel it but can't put my finger on it.

Kate Do you suppose he knows about us?

Joss No...No...It's not that! *[Wipes his forehead with handkerchief]* It's become clammy all of a sudden. I think there's thunder in the air.

[Goes towards exit]

Kate The barometer is steady and the forecast is good.

Joss Yes, I know. But no matter how steady things may seem, you must always make allowance for the local storm.

[Exit Joss]

[End of Scene 1 of Act 1]

ACT ONE

SCENE TWO

[THAT NIGHT
Chinese lanterns and naked bulbs light the garden.
Enter Joss followed by Ellie]

Joss I don't *love* the summer, although I like to spend as much time as I can out of doors. Give me an October evening up in any room. I like it just before the dark. To sit by the window and watch the clouds roll by - swirling, tumbling clouds - the kind of clouds you think you could touch if you put your hand out - clouds without shape. After your mother died, they were the only consolation I had and they were consolation. A man could lose himself in the comfort of their great movements. Thunder and violence--without noise or tension. That's what they were. I used to sit and think until it was dark, but then, because I had grown used to the dark, I could distinguish the movements and you know something, Ellie…*[Ellie takes his arm]* …I was comforted, strangely comforted.

Ellie I understand, Dad. You felt as if the fingers of those clouds caressed you, soothed you and told you that suffering must be borne.

Joss *[Astonished]* Not quite, but you're right. Life isn't full of clouds and isn't full of sunshine.

Ellie You were praying, Dad.

Joss Praying?

Ellie You were praying, because any man who can devote so many hours to a sky created by God is surely praying...*[Cheerfully]* I love the clouds too when they toss and gallop like work horses who have been let loose in the fields...

Joss That's a good description...very good.

Ellie And I love it out-of-doors when the wind is blowing and puffing and every home is happy. Daddy, do you think I'm honest?

[She takes a bottle of lager from a case under the table]

Joss I think so. *[Ellie uncorks and pours lager for him]* Now, what am I being held up for? A new dress? I think I've got it. This is new, but it's a nice form of hold-up. Get around the doting old father by pouring his beer and listening to his rambling. I'm beginning to think we both owe the clouds a lot. *[Mock-sigh]* What is it this time?

Ellie *[Handing him glass of beer]* Sit down.

Joss *[Sits]* And boss him affectionately, too.

Ellie Are you comfortable?

Joss   All right. Let's have it! This is the second time this has happened today. Now, suppose you come straight to the point and tell me what it's all about?

Ellie   I'm going to be a nun.

Joss   This is excellent lager. So you're going to be a nun? So is every girl of nineteen who's beginning to learn the cruel realities. Or did I hear you right? Did you say nun?

Ellie   Yes, Dad … nun. Do I have your blessing?

Joss   Sorry, Ellie!…You're too young to know your own mind fully. I've nothing against nuns but, Goddammit, I'm not going to have a daughter of mine throwing her life away. I want grandchildren, hundreds of 'em, and you want children, too, only you don't know it yet.

Ellie   Yes… but they must be children who need me desperately. Other people's. People's who don't care enough.

Joss   My dear and lovely daughter, it's the function of a woman to have babies. When you were little more than a baby yourself you were pushing a pram with a doll in it. Isn't that the natural approach to natural motherhood.

Ellie   I'm joining the Salutation Order. You should be flattered that they're going to accept me.

Joss   I'm not worried ... you'll change your mind when some handsome young fellow loses his head over you.

Ellie   No, I won't...I'm going in September.

Joss   You mean it?

Ellie   Yes, Daddy, I mean it.

Joss   God!

Ellie   It's what I want to be.

Joss   Then I suppose I'd better think about it. The clothes are more modern now, aren't they?

Ellie   So I'm told.

Joss   I'm not surprised. You were a lovely child, Ellie, and you're a lovely girl. It's a pity you don't know more boys. This is all terribly sudden.

[Enter Kate]

Kate   Anybody for soup?

Ellie   I know more boys than you think. Ask Kate.

Joss   *[Mock-indignant]* Is this true?

Kate   *[Mock-sadness]* Every word of it! Phone-calls, letters...don't talk to me. Now, who wants soup or coffee or sandwiches?

Ellie   Let's wait for the boys.

Kate   There! I told you! She wouldn't enjoy it if the boys weren't here. *[Exit Kate]*

Ellie   Do you remember, a while ago I asked you if you thought I was honest?

Joss   *[Seriously]* I know of nobody more so.

Ellie   I want to be.

Joss   Well, then, be honest.

Ellie   I know about you and Kate.

Joss   *[Unnerved]* You know what?

Ellie   About you and Kate.

Joss   *[Flustered]* What are you talking about?

Ellie   I've known for a while, and I'm happy because it means you'll have somebody to look after you when I'm gone.

Joss   You know, and you approve?

Ellie   Of course, I approve.

Joss   *[Puts an arm about her]* You're a remarkable girl.

Ellie   Marry Kate, Dad, as soon as possible.

Joss   It's not so easy. The boys have to be considered.

Ellie Tell them. They're not boys any longer. They're grown men. Besides, they're fond of Kate. You're taking her to Blane on Sunday, aren't you?

Joss Yes.

Ellie Tell them when you come back. I'll do the softening up while you're away.

Joss It won't be easy.

Ellie Anything worthwhile is never easy…that sounds like Toddy. If I were you, I'd tell Toddy now. One at a time.

Joss Not a hope. I'd be embarrassed.

Ellie Right, so! When you come back from Blane on Sunday.

[Enter Toddy. He takes off his coat and throws it across a chair].

Toddy Do me a favour, Ellie. Pour me a nice cool bottle of lager. *(Ellie locates same under table and pours)* it must be the warmest summer in living memory.

Joss 'Forty-six was warmer. Even the farmers complained. I remember an excruciating night of that year. It was in Crosshaven. The only time I ever struck a man. There was a crowd of us in a pub. Monsignor O'Leary was in my company and there was a discussion about the Blessed Trinity…This man got up. I think he was from Kansas…

Ellie Dad!

Joss Sorry, Ellie, I ramble too much.

Toddy Is Jamesy in?

Joss Not yet! He should be here any minute now. We have an appointment…'Forty-six was an enormous year. A funny thing…I hope you'll forgive me, Ellie…I think that was the year the more modern-minded Irishwoman started to wear panties. It was bloomers and knickers before that … horrible bloody elastic knickers down to their knees. They kept out the cold, of course.

Toddy Listen to him…the cold technical draper's approach to underwear.

Ellie *[Hands Toddy his lager]* I'll get some ice in the kitchen.

[Exit Ellie]

Toddy Young Bennett's in hospital.

Joss Crash his car?

Toddy No… no…nothing like that.

Joss Is he ill?

Toddy He's ill, all right!

Joss You sound very smug. Has he got somebody in a bit of bother?

Toddy Well, let's say that if he kept away from a certain young lady he'd be on his feet. *[Both laugh]*

Joss Like father, like son. Oul' Bennett would screw a midge in his time.

Toddy That's what the boss told me to-day. Hard to believe it, looking at old Bennett now. Looks like a Church deacon.

Joss And acts like one! The parish priest is afraid of his life of him. Told me so himself.

Toddy Here's Ellie.

[Enter Ellie, with container of ice. She plops some into Toddy's lager]

Ellie Enough?

Toddy Bags of it, thanks!

Joss Are you aware of the fact that your charming sister will be leaving us soon?

Toddy *[Splutters his lager]* Leaving us?

Joss She's going in the nuns.

Toddy The nuns?…Oh, no!

Ellie What's the matter? You'd think I was disgracing the family.

Toddy Leaving it all behind…I think I'll bring you to the

Boat Club Dance next week.

Joss She's serious, Toddy.

Toddy I know bloody well she is. That's why I'm joking… It's the surprise.

Ellie You should be delighted.

Toddy I am, Ellie, but let it sink in first. I suppose we should be proud, really, but it seems such a waste. *[Consternation]* You won't be going before my marriage?

Ellie I'll be here…my last public appearance.

Toddy We'll be able to visit you, I hope?

Ellie It's the Salutation Order.

Toddy Thank God for that! For a moment I thought you might become one of those strange little women who never see the light of day.

Joss The Poor Clares! Ah, Goddammit, that's too far. I wouldn't permit it.

Ellie Yes, you would, if I made up my mind to go.

Joss My only daughter turning into a nun. Oh, dear, what next?

Toddy You could be ordained a priest.

Joss *[Taken aback for a moment]* Now, that's going a bit too far. Anyway, I've no Latin.

Toddy You don't need Latin. What you need is a good housekeeper.

Ellie Another lager, Dad?

Joss No, thanks, Ellie, I've had two already.

Toddy Has Jamesy spoken to you yet, Dad?

Joss No, he hasn't. Maybe you know what's going on?

Toddy I have a fair idea. But I think he wants to tell you himself.

Joss Goddammit, what's all the mystery about?.

Toddy You'll know soon enough. That's his car now.

Ellie What's going on?...I know...Jamesy is renovating the shop again and he wants Dad's approval.

Joss No. It's not that. He can build a skyscraper as far as I'm concerned. It's his business now. I'm retired, remember.

Toddy His car was outside the "Rob Roy". He probably has a few taken, Dad. It isn't easy for him just now.

Joss Yes, Tod.

Toddy It's just one of those things. You'll understand when he tells you. I'm positive you will.

Joss   I hope he isn't drunk. Has he been drinking heavily lately?

Toddy   *[Pause]* Not heavily, but more than usual.

Joss   Goddammit, you have me dead keen to find out what it's all about.

Ellie   There he is now.

[Toddy rises, finishes his lager and puts empty glasses on the table. Enter Jamesy to be greeted with silence. Jamesy throws off his coat and immediately selects a bottle of lager from the box.]

Jamesy   Where's the opener?

Ellie   Give it to me. I'll pour it.

Jamesy   *[Hands the lager to Ellie]* Boy, what a scorching day! Must be the hottest summer in living memory.

Toddy   That's what I said, but Dad says 'forty-six.

Jamesy   'Forty-six? I can't remember 'forty-six too well but, my God, it must have been hot if it was hotter than this. I'll have to take your word for it. This year it's hot enough for me.

Joss   'Forty-seven beat the lot! We had a chalet in Crosshaven that year. All three of you were as brown as berries. There were a number of boys and girls arrested for nude swimming in one of the coves. Goddammit, it was hard to blame them. It made newspaper headlines at the time. *[To boys]* Thank God, you were more interested in the Sports Page. A scandalous year.

Toddy I remember it! Oul' Bennett spotted them through his telescope. 'Twas all the talk.

Joss Oul' Bennett's famous telescope!

Toddy It's a wonder nobody ever socked him.

Jamesy A good hard kick in the arse is what he wanted.

Joss Let's get down to cases. Jamesy, sit over here.

[Jamesy obeys, taking his drink along].

Joss *[Good-naturedly]* I understand you have something on your mind? Toddy knows, and I don't know how many more. Don't you think it's my turn?

Toddy *[To Ellie]* Come on! I'll walk you to the end of the garden and show you some leprechauns.

Ellie Leprechauns!…I want to stay and listen.

Toddy There are leprechauns around all right. I saw some droppings yesterday.

Joss Leprechauns' droppings! Be good for the export market.

Toddy   Put them in plastic bags with four-leaved shamrocks.

Joss   "Genuine Irish Leprechauns Droppings!" Fresh as the morning dew!

Toddy   Two dollars and fifty cents a packet! *[To Ellie]* Come on love. The night is wasting. *[To Jamesy - seriously]* Good luck, Jamesy.

[Exit Ellie and Toddy]

Jamesy   Did Toddy give you any hint?

Joss   No, ... only, whatever it is, he knew about it before me.

Jamesy   Did Toddy give you any hint?

Joss   You asked me to-day, is it something to do with a girl...

[Enter Toddy hurriedly]

Toddy   *[Nodding sympathetically to Jamesy]* Sorry for butting in, gents! Jamesy! Penny is coming on the 4.45 tomorrow evening and I won't be able to meet her. Would you oblige...I'll be half an hour late...I have to look over some property for a client.

Jamesy   Of course! 4.45, you say?

Toddy   Thanks a million... Ellie and I are going as far as the river.

[Exit Toddy]

Joss *[To Jamesy]* Now, Goddammit, isn't it about time you told me?

Jamesy About this girl…

Joss What girl?

Jamesy This girl I'm going to tell you about.

Joss Your girl-friend.

Jamesy No, Dad, not my girl-friend. This girl is pregnant.

Joss *[Coldly]* Go on!

Jamesy What do you mean, go on? I've just told you.

Joss Are you responsible?

Jamesy I suppose so.

Joss Make up your mind! Are you, or aren't you?

Jamesy As far as I know, I am. But what's got into you?

Joss Anybody else involved?

Jamesy I don't think so.

Joss Are you sure?

Jamesy Yes, …I don't know…I'm not sure…I suppose I'm sure…How the hell do I know?…Well, come on!

Start giving out the pay.

Joss I'm a little dumbfounded, Jamesy. I've often prepared myself for a situation like this. I've rehearsed it more than once but *[Laughs, falsely]* I've forgotten the lines…as if there were lines. I can tell you, however, I've long ago decided what my stand would be if it happened and it *has* happened, hasn't it? Hasn't it, Jamesy? And a firm stand is needed, one way or the other.

Jamesy Yes, Dad. I'm sorry I've left you down. It was…it was…I didn't really want it. It was sordid and dirty. My imagination was the whole cause. Dirty, lunatic imagination when I couldn't sleep.

Joss *[Looks after Ellie and Toddy]* Toddy knows. He knew before me, not that it matters. He knows?

Jamesy Yes.

Joss Ellie's going in the nuns.

Jamesy What?

Joss Yes. She announced it this evening. If she knew this!

Jamesy She doesn't have to know. That would be a lousy trick, telling her. That would be cruel.

Joss She's one of the family…your sister. We don't seem to be on the same wavelength, boy.

Jamesy God! Say something, Dad! I'm waiting for your verdict.

Joss To me there is no problem. It is quite simple. You'll marry the girl.

Jamesy *[Hits table and rises]* I will not! Do you think I'm a fool.

Joss *[Calmly]* You're anything but a fool. I'm thinking of you, Jamesy, and this unfortunate girl and the child she's going to have. Can you stand there and tell me that you want your child to be nameless and less fortunate than you?

Jamesy *[Long-drawn-out sigh]* You can hardly expect me to feel concern for something I've never seen.

Joss How naive can you be, man? The child is yours… nothing can change that.

Jamesy It happens every day of the week.

Joss You prefer to call it an accident?

Jamesy It certainly wasn't deliberate. I know I've done wrong, Dad, and I'm genuinely sorry, but it's happened to thousands like me.

Joss If you know you've done wrong, then you know what you must do. Restitution is the answer.

Jamesy Restitution! Is this your restitution - life imprisonment?

Joss   You think that now...you have no idea how time passes.

Jamesy   Toddy is going to see the girl and her parents.

Joss   Is that the property he said he was going to look over, and while he's doing your dirty work, you're picking up his girl.

Jamesy   He's my brother and he's my solicitor. It's his job. You're not with the times, Dad. You know how many girls went to England to have babies last year- seven hundred...there are houses there which cater for this sort of thing, and the kids get into good homes.

Joss   Yes... and all because of the concerted actions of seven hundred cowards like you.

Jamesy   I'm not a coward. It's the right way out, the only thing to do for a man in my position.

Joss   It'll still be your child.

Jamesy   Not when it's adopted by somebody else.

Joss   You'll carry the guilt, Jamesy. You'll always have the hangdog look, the apologetic air. I've seen it. They never live it down and it's worse with the years. Do the right thing! Marry the girl. Give it a chance and 'twill work! You have no other way out.

Jamesy *[Finality]* Not a hope! Anyway, there's another girl. We have an understanding.

Joss *[Laughs]* God…you're a comical man! Another girl. This is the airs-and-graces one, I take it… the nice one. I want you to think it over, Jamesy. It's your duty to marry the first girl and I'm going to see that you do your duty.

Jamesy Try to understand, Dad.

Joss I've heard enough for one sitting.

Jamesy And so have I! I was honest enough to tell you everything.

Joss To get my approval.

Jamesy Interpret it whatever way you like, but you won't find me confiding in you again.

Joss As you wish.

Jamesy You're a narrow-minded old man, without the slightest bit of humanity.

Joss If you mean I'm a man who knows when one of his sons is guilty of a crime, you're right. I've done my utmost to give you a good Catholic upbringing. You should do your duty as a Catholic.

Jamesy Oh, stop preaching and come down to earth…what's the matter with you? *[Exciting]* …Weren't there any bastards in your time?

[Exit Jamesy]

Joss   There might have been, if I had neglected to marry your mother.

[End of Act One]

ACT TWO

SCENE ONE

[Action as before
TIME is the following afternoon.
Three or four sheets hang from a clothesline near back wall.
Joss is seated at a table, repairing a fishing rod.]
[Enter Kate]

Joss I thought I might take a few casts on Sunday while we're at Blane.

Kate The water is low.

Joss I know where to look. If the tide's right there will be sea-trout.

Kate I couldn't look at 'em.

Joss That's because you come from generations of poachers. You ate too many when you were a child. You're surfeited…but I'm not.

Kate I hope these sheets are aired properly. *[She lowers basket and feels sheets]* They seem all right. I need pillow slips.

Joss Jamsey can get those for you in the shop.

Kate   I've got some but they're threadbare…About Jamsey,

Joss   Have you spoken to him since last night?

Joss   Yes, I asked him to pass the marmalade this morning. "Sure Dad!" he said, as if nothing had happened. You'd think we'd never spoken last night. What's the matter with the younger generation? They adapt so quickly, it's almost unnatural.

Kate   We never see things the way children do.

Joss   You mean, they don't see things the way we do.

Kate   Jamesy is still a bit of a child.

Joss   Jamesy is not a child. He's Managing Director of a damn good business. He should know his responsibilities.

Kate   He doesn't want to fight with you, that's clear. *[Takes sheets from line]* The way I see it, every young lad up to the age of thirty has a lot of the baby left in him.

Joss   I know that. And I don't want to fight with him. There was never a word between us 'till this thing happened. He should know that, in his position, he can't afford to mix with girls like that.

Kate   Help me take this line down. *[JOSS does so]* I don't want to take sides. I never have. You know that. But aren't you being a bit hard on him?

Joss I'm not!

Kate It's often wise to close one's eyes at times.

Joss You mean, it's often easier.

Kate Why don't you just forget what he's done? He's sorry.

Joss You too! Toddy said exactly the same thing this morning. Jamesy has made it hard for himself. Nobody seems to understand what's involved here.

Kate Now! Now! There, but for the grace of God…

Joss I know! I know! But surely you don't approve…

Kate Me?…Approve?…God, I think it's awful, but he's your son. He's got your name and he's boss of a big business. He never promised to marry her, you know. Now, if they had been going steady or if they had been engaged…But this is different. You can't expect a boy like Jamesy, with the whole world before him, to make such a sacrifice, just because some girl got a notion of him and led him on.

Joss But what about the girl? Hadn't she the whole world before her too?…Who is she anyway? Do you know her?

Kate Her name is Monahan. She lives about twenty miles from here. She's nineteen. She works as a domestic… or, rather, she did. She's at home at the moment.

Joss   Poor, unlucky child! She's out there thinking it's the end of the world and here's our Jamesy preparing to marry a debutante.

Kate   It's unfortunate.

Joss   How come he never brought her here…never once… she wasn't good enough, of course. Obviously he was ashamed of her. But not ashamed to be intimate with her. No … that was alright…that was fine.

Kate   Look, Joss! He saw her home one night after a dance. He saw her once again after another dance and that was that. If it wasn't Jamesy it would have been somebody else.

Joss   But it was our Jamesy: You all seem to keep forgetting that.

Kate   He's a good mark, Joss. Most girls of her class would be honoured.

Joss   That's no excuse. And class has nothing to do with it.

Kate   If he's made to marry her, 'twill finish him. And what of Toddy's girl? What about her people? And Ellie about to enter a convent. The whole city would be counting the months and days after they got married. People do that-even the most respectable people. It's a passion with them and they laugh and snigger when they're proved right. Besides, Jamesy's going steady now.

Joss So I gather. Who is she?

Kate Her father is Managing Director of an advertising firm.

Joss And is *she* pregnant?

Kate JOSS!

Joss It all boils down to a simple fact. He wants to marry a girl he doesn't have to marry and he's ruining the life of the girl he should marry.

Kate You make it all sound so simple!

Joss [*Goes to Exit*] I've heard all the arguments and I can tell you this. No child of my son's or, if you like, no grandchild of mine is going to go through life without my label on his back.

[Exit JOSS. Kate sighs and stands for a brief moment. Enter Ellie.]

Ellie What's the matter with *him?*

Kate Nothing that concerns you, Ellie.

Ellie Let me guess! I've got it! You've had a lovers' tiff. The course of true love…

Kate [*Smacks Ellie's behind playfully*] You know too much, you do!

Ellie Do you know what time it is?

Kate   Oh, dear! I'd forgotten.

Ellie   It's ten to five. The train's been in for five minutes. That means they'll be here in another five.

Kate   And I here, prattling with you, when I should be upstairs getting the room ready.

Ellie   Not so fast!.. *[Calls her father]* Daddy! Come in here!...*[To Kate]* You stand right where you are.

[Enter a dark-faced JOSS]

Joss   Now, what's the matter?

Ellie   First of all, a smile from my little boy...Smile!

[JOSS smiles in spite of himself. Ellie perches herself on the table between them]

Ellie   Down to brass tacks, as they say.

Kate   Oh, dear! I should have gone when the going was good.

Ellie   I want you two to fix a date for the wedding.

Joss   The sooner the better.

Ellie   Now when you come back from Blane to-morrow night I'll have a little party going, cosy and intimate...

Kate   She's as cracked as the crows. I always suspected it; now I know it.

Ellie   We'll have Toddy and Toddy's girl, and Jamesy and Jamesy's girl and myself, and the pair of you when you get back. I could begin, by way of no harm and say-quite casually of course-"Where have you two lovebirds been all day?" And then you, Pops...you very calmly announce that you and Kate are thinking of getting married before I go into the Con- vent as it wouldn't be proper for the two of you to live here alone in your present state; and when I hear the news I'll scream with delight and surprise and announce how pleased we are, one and all. Why-we could have a double wedding, or a treble wedding.

Joss   A splendid idea. You've got a sound head on those nice shoulders of yours.

Kate   I'm not sure that it's the right time.

Ellie   Will you listen to her? Trying to cheat me out of a stepmother. You'll do as I say, Pops. It's the last chance I'll have of making a match.

Kate   Couldn't we postpone it for a while?

Ellie   No, we couldn't. It's settled now.

Kate   But Toddy and Jamesy...what will they think?

Ellie   They didn't consult you about *their* marriage plans. Why should you consult them?...There's the car!

Kate   *[Seizes her basket]* Let me out of here. *[To Ellie]* Don't show her to her room till I come down, will you?

Ellie Don't worry! I'll stand by you, Kate.

Kate I'd rather be entertaining a bishop than a strange girl.

[Exit Kate]

Ellie *[To JOSS]* Don't look so smug...I haven't finished with you!

Joss What have I done now?

Ellie In bed last night, Dad, I was thinking...

Joss *[Evasively]* You want me to teach you how to drive? No...you want one last fling before you enter?

Ellie No...it isn't that, Daddy. Do you know how long it is since we said the Rosary in this house...all of us together, I mean? Not since last May, the last Sunday night an May and even then there were only three of us...Toddy and Jamesy were late.

Joss You're right as usual. It's a long time. It's too long. We'll start soon again.

Ellie We'd better or I'll withdraw my guns tomorrow night and leave you in the front line all by yourself.

Joss *[Puts his arm around her]* You don't have to threaten me, Ellie. We shouldn't have overlooked it for so long. It's my fault of course, and nobody else's.

Ellie Here they come! I hope she's not one of those lofty types.

[Enter Jamesy]

Jamesy She's a peach! Wait till you see her. Come on out, Penny!

[Enter Penny. She is a distinguished good-looking girl in her early twenties]

Jamesy Penny, this is Ellie, and this is Dad.

[Ellie hurries forward and kisses Penny]

Joss Step aside! Let me shake hands with my daughter-in-law to be. *[JOSS takes both her hands]* I can't tell you how welcome you are, Penny, and how happy I am for Toddy. Come and sit down. You must be tired after your journey. Sit here near me.

Ellie Oh, no, you don't…she sits near me.

Penny *[Notices fishing-rod on table]* Is this Toddy's?

Joss No! This is a trout rod made from greenheart. Toddy is a deep-sea fisherman. He keeps his gear in his room. Sacred stuff!

Penny *[Laughs]* I know! He told me.

Ellie Are you interested in fishing, Penny?

Penny   Not any more! I've landed the one fish I wanted. *[All laugh]*

Joss   A cool drink?

Penny   No, thanks, I couldn't touch a thing. But you go and have one if you want it.

Joss   Sit down and tell me all about yourself. How did you come to meet our Toddy?

Ellie   Give her a chance, Dad.

Joss   But I'm curious and I can't wait.

Penny   At the County Hunt Ball. He was with another girl. I soon put a stop to that.

[All laugh]

Joss   Just like that!

Penny   Just like that!

Joss   I'm so pleased. I couldn't have done better if I'd selected you myself. He's a lucky fellow.

Penny   It's the other way around. I'm the lucky one.

Ellie   Oh, you must never say that! What would the men think?

[All laugh]

Jamesy I'll take the bag upstairs, and put the car in. See you later Penny.

Penny Sure, James, and thanks for meeting me.

Jamesy Oh, that! Any time! It was a pleasure.

[Exit Jamesy]

Penny Jamesy is so charming. You've got a lovely family, Mr. O'Brien.

Joss Joss! You must call me Joss.

Penny Alright, then, I'll call you Joss.

Joss Good! Now, how long are you going to stay?

Penny I've got to be back on Monday evening.

Joss and Ellie Oh, no!

Ellie So soon?

Joss It's hardly worth your while. You'll stay a week and we're not taking any excuses, are we, Ellie?

Ellie Certainly not!

Penny But I've got to be back. Daddy and Mummy are going on a holiday. I promised.

Joss Oh, well, if you promised your father and mother, we won't hold you, but you'll come for a longer holiday before the wedding.

Penny That's a promise.

Joss Good! And the next time I'll drive up for you.

Ellie That would be great. Toddy is working very hard lately.

Penny He'll have a wife to support shortly.

Joss His practice is taking shape. It was tough at first.

Penny Yes, I know. He told me how good you were to him.

Joss Oh, that was nothing!...But let's talk about you- After you met at the Hunt Ball, what then?

Ellie Isn't he nosey?

Penny Aren't they all? *[All laugh]* After the Hunt Ball...let me see...Of course we just met that night, although we did have three dances...

Joss Well, you wouldn't mind one dance...

Ellie Or two dances...

ALL But three!

Penny About a week after the Hunt Ball he rang me.

Joss He waited a whole week?

Penny No. A day...but I wasn't in.

Ellie   You were out, naturally.

Penny   How did you guess?

Ellie   It's easy! *[Both girls laugh]*

Penny   Well, he asked me for a date and I said I didn't know, but then I said yes, in case he might change his mind. He asked me if I liked Races and I told him I just loved them…never missed them. Of course, I'd never been to a race-meeting before, just couldn't care less although Dad keeps a few hunters. So he took me to the Races and he proposed that night while we were having dinner.

Ellie   Which course?

Penny   Why, I believe it was the Fish.

[Enter Kate. Joss immediately goes to her].

Joss   Penny, I want you to meet Kate, our housekeeper. She's one of the family.

[Penny rises and shakes Kate's hand]

Penny   Toddy told me all about you. You've set quite a standard for me.

Kate   It's a pleasure to welcome you, Miss Penny.

Joss   It's "Penny", Kate…not "Miss Penny". Just plain Penny, although she's anything but plain, I can tell you.

Penny I'm sure you'll tell me all about Toddy's fads, Kate.

Kate He hates parsnips, Brussels sprouts and turnips.

Kate If his collars aren't stiff you'll know the reason why

Penny Well, those are worthwhile tips. Anything else? And he likes a change of socks every day.

Penny Please tell me more.

Kate He likes gravy. Give him enough gravy and you'll have him eating out of the palm of your hand.

Penny Well, I'll certainly remember that.

Ellie Come on, I'll show you to your room. You'll like it. You can see the river.

[Ellie takes Penny by hand. They are about to exit].

Penny *[To Ellie]* You go ahead. I'll be right with you.

[Exit Ellie. Penny takes a banknote from her purse and hands it to Kate]

Penny Thanks for getting my room ready. Buy yourself a little present with this.

[Exit Penny. Kate stares, dumbfounded, at the note in her hand and, after a pause, says]

Kate Well, I've certainly been put in my place, haven't I?

Joss Oh, now, she didn't mean anything by that. Just thought it was the right thing to do.

Kate In that case, why didn't she give it to you or to Ellie? I've always had enough. All belong to me had enough. We were never short of anything in Blane.

[Exit Kate. JOSS is left scratching his head in perplexity. Enter Jamesy]

Jamesy What's the matter with Kate?

Joss How the hell should I know? What's the matter with everyone? Have you thought about what you should do?

Jamesy *[Cheerfully …rubs his palms together]* Yes … my mind is made up.

Joss Good! I hope it's the right thing.

Jamesy As far as I'm concerned, it is. It's the right thing for me.

Joss So that's the way of it?

Jamesy It's the only way.

Joss She's the same age as Ellie, isn't she? Did she remind you of Ellie?

Jamesy That's not fair, Dad.

Joss You'll marry that unfortunate girl, Jamesy, and

that's the end of it.

Jamesy Sorry, Dad…I'm marrying somebody else.

Joss I'll put a stop to that!

Jamesy How?

Joss By having a little talk with your intended, that's how!

Jamesy She already knows. She's the first person I told.

Joss Good God!…And she's still willing to marry you?

Jamesy Of course she is! She's human enough to overlook one foolish mistake!

Joss One foolish mistake!

Jamesy She believes a man should sow his wild oats before he gets married, not afterwards.

Joss And Toddy's girl, Penny?

Jamesy I'm sure Toddy's told her.

Joss And she doesn't mind?

Jamesy Why should *she* mind. It's got nothing to do with her.

Joss Of course not! She's not the one who's pregnant.

Jamesy They're all willing to overlook what's past, except you. I've put the past behind me. I can be a good father and a good husband. I want to, Dad.

Joss But, Jamesy, you're already a father or about to be.

Jamesy Without losing my temper, Dad...like I said, it's a thing of the past. I'll thank you not to bring up the subject again.

Joss Is this real? What's happening here? I don't believe it! I don't believe that a son of mine could turn out like this.

Jamesy *[Violently]* In the name of God, you ould fool, will you face reality. Do you want to ruin me, to smash me completely. Is that what you want? What kind of an idiot are you and what kind of an idiot do you take me for? I'm not going to tear my whole future to pieces because I once.... just once.... gratified a sudden whim, a stupid vulgar whim that means damn-all when it was done...I'm sorry...I'm sorry it's like this between us...But I'll be damned if I'm going to marry a semi-illiterate skivvy to satisfy you. Believe me, I'm sorry it turned out this way.

Joss *[Moves towards exit]* I know you're sorry...and you look sorry...in fact you're the sorriest looking sonovabitch I ever saw in my whole life.

[Exit JOSS]

Jamesy *[Weakly]* Dad...Dad...Don't forsake me, Dad...

Please, Dad...Try to understand...I couldn't help myself...

[He covers his face with his hands and sits weakly on a chair]

[End of Scene 1 of Act 2]

ACT TWO

SCENE TWO

[Action as before.
THE TIME is the following [SUNDAY] night.
ELLIE and PENNY sit in the garden. A bell rings in the distance.
ELLIE scrutinises her watch.]

Ellie Nine on the dot! Always on the Ball!...But, where was I...Oh, yes! Toddy was a scream...He stayed out all one night and Daddy rang the police, thinking he might be drowned. He was eighteen then. I remember it so well. Talk about commotion. The police alerted the Lifeboat...and who staggered in, drunk, at two o'clock in the morning?...

Penny Toddy?

Ellie Yes, Toddy, singing at the top of his voice. But don't tell him I told you. You'll get it out of him in due course. It was the first time he got drunk, and the last time...except for being merry a few times in between. And then...*(Chokes with laughter)* ... and the time he let the Book fall when he was an Altarboy...He picked it up as if nothing had happened...I thought I'd faint there and then. Everybody thought he'd surely go for the Church but then, a few Sundays after the Book incident, he refused to go behind the

Altar ever again and said he wanted to be like Dad and marry a girl like Mammy. God rest her. Oh, he was a scream…They always go to the pub like this…most Sunday nights anyway. I'm glad you understand.

Penny Of course!

Ellie That's how I hear all the local news. The boys bring it back from the pub.

Penny My father always says: "What has a man, apart from his wife and family, except the company of his friends?" He says the pub is the only place where he can meet the few friends he has left.

Ellie You know, Penny, I've loved our bit of a talk.

Penny So have I! When we're married, we'll come to see you in the convent. We'll come often. We must never lose touch, now that we've met and liked each other.

Ellie Will you, Penny? I'd love it if you did…you and Toddy.

Penny It's what you want… to be a nun, I mean. Isn't it, Ellie?

Ellie Yes, more than all the world.

Penny I thought about it for a while. I suppose every girl does. A young doctor did locum in the village. I was eighteen and I fell madly in love with him. Then his fiancée came for a weekend. They were so happy together…

Ellie   So!

Penny   So I decided to enter a convent.

[Both enjoy this]

Ellie   Before the boys come in, let's go and change. I have so many dresses I'll never wear. They're yours after I go, if you want them. Try one to-night, just for fun.

Penny   I'd love to…to surprise Toddy.

Ellie   Oh, he'll love it. They'll bring back a crate of beer and there will be a song or two. Do you like a sing-song?

Penny   I love a song…to join in, that is, but I hope nobody asks me to sing solo.

Ellie   I'll see to that. Daddy is a nice singer and so is Toddy, and Jamesy, too, when he gets going. Oh…Oh…here they come. Our bonny boys. Did Toddy tell you he plays the guitar?

Penny   Yes.

Ellie   He's not very good.

[They both laugh]

Ellie   They're in the house. Nine o'clock they said and nine o'clock it is.

[Enter Toddy and Jamesy. They carry a crate of lager between them].

Jamesy   Ah, the ladies! I think there's enough beer. There's gin cooling an the fridge all day, if anyone wants it.

[Meanwhile Toddy is kissing Penny]

Ellie   Let's go, Penny…

[Penny breaks away from Toddy and joins Ellie]

Toddy   Where are you going?

Ellie   We are going to make ourselves even more beautiful.

[They both exit laughing]

Jamesy   Let's have a lager.

Toddy   Good idea!

[He uncorks two bottles and they quaff without the aid of glasses]

Toddy   Why didn't you bring Marcella tonight?

Jamesy   Are you serious? You know the way the old man is at the moment?

Toddy   He wouldn't have said anything…not in the presence of Ellie and Penny.

Jamesy   You may be right but I daren't risk an outburst, not in front of Ellie. Tell me about yesterday again.

Toddy   I told you all.

Jamesy   Tell me again.

Toddy   I got to the village about three o'clock, enquired where the house was and located it...no bother. There wasn't anybody in, so I snooped around and found them, in a small meadow behind the house...

Jamesy   The whole family?

Toddy   She was there and her brother and her father and mother. She sat on the headland. The other three were saving hay. She was pathetic, Jamesy, a fat, drowsy little figure, thrown back against the summer hay. The father and mother came over and I explained my case. They took the cheque quickly enough. The brother stood brooding a few yards away. She's off to England tomorrow...they can't get rid of her fast enough...worried in case the neighbours get suspicious. You're lucky you're not marrying into that bunch. The girl looked nice enough, but she never opened her mouth, not once, not even when the old man folded the cheque and put it into his waistcoat pocket.

Jamesy   And the brother?

Toddy   Well, as I told you, just as I was about to leave he came near me. "I'd love to kick the guts out of you!" he said. It was you he meant...or was it? He could have, too, because I had extremely poor grounds for defence. The old man and the old woman restrained him. Then the old man showed him the cheque but he struck it from their hands and stalked across the fields.

Jamesy And that was that!

Toddy That was that. I didn't like it. I deal with muck every day of the week but, somehow, this…this sickened me. I wouldn't do it for anybody else.

Jamesy Thanks, Toddy! Well, it's all over now.

Toddy Don't ever mess around again! If you do, I'll wash my hands of you and you know me well enough to know that I mean it.

Jamesy It won't happen again, I assure you.

Toddy Marcella is right for you. I like her. She's your own class. By the way…a question…how many times? I mean those other girls.

Jamesy I don't know. [*Pause*] Twenty-five. Thirty. More maybe. I'm not sure- I try to count them sometimes but I feel so guilty, I stop.

Toddy And your pals?

Jamesy Much the same.

Toddy Twenty-five to thirty…it's about par for the course, then.

Jamesy You're too straitlaced and too upright: that's what's wrong with you. I should have taken you under my wing. You're older…but you're younger in so many ways. So's Dad.

Toddy You mean, I was never initiated.

Jamesy Well, sort of. Nearly everybody agrees that it's necessary to have at least one woman before settling down.

Toddy Too late now!

Jamesy Yes, I suppose it is.

Toddy It almost frightens me that I should be a freak.

Jamesy Come on! Have another beer.

Toddy Now, that's the first sensible thing you've said tonight…get me a glass, will you, and do something sensible for a change.

[Jamesy locates a pair of glasses and starts to pour. Hands glass to Toddy]

Jamesy What's the matter with you?

Toddy Reminiscing.

Jamesy About what…and when…and where?

Toddy Oh!…Micky Sullivan. Micky was the youngest of a family of eighteen.

Jamesy Micky, eh?

Toddy I met him a month ago, did I tell you?

Jamesy No.

Toddy Micky hadn't a spatter. I remember his mother once sent him for a chamber-pot. I was with him. "What size do you want?" the clerk asked him. That stumped him for a minute, but only for a minute. "Give me a pot," said Micky, "That'll hold the water of twenty". He has five kids. Five! Still the same job, travelling for Cant and Company. And Willie St. George, Father Willie. I think he's in Lima now. I must find out. And Harpy…Harpy Dwyer.., Harpy went to America. Harpy was the most innocent boy I ever knew and the funniest.

Jamesy Harpy was a howl.

Toddy You must have had a right laugh at us then.

Jamesy No. No.

Toddy There were you and the boys living it up, chasing skivvies and exchanging the names of good things, and…D'you remember? We thought we were the happiest chaps on the face of creation; up the river on Sundays singing *"Dee-olee-ay"* and *"Swanee"*. D'you know that Harpy hitch-hiked to Dublin to buy the sheet-music of *"Patsy Fagan"*? Imagine! The sheet- music of *"Patsy Fagan"*? Maybe we were all wrong. Used you and the boys laugh at us?

Jamesy *[Pause]* No, Toddy…Never!…If we did, it never rang true, because the truth is that we envied you.

Toddy You remember that tall, cadaverous fellow…I saw him once or twice at College, after.

Jamesy Yes, Ollie Sheave.

Toddy He was a low type. You remember him?

Jamesy *[Uncertainly]* Y-e-s! Yes. I remember.

Toddy Always on about skivs or shopgirls and miscarriages and once about a poor girl who had a dead-born baby under a hedge in a field. What a lot of sniggering there was, and how everybody respected his views… *[Seizes bottle from table and advances on Jamesy]* …I've often felt like killing him since. I've done it in my mind and, as Christ is my judge, I could break this bottle over your head now…*[Jamesy backs away fearfully]* …to smash and kep on smashing until I get the guilt out of my system. *[Relaxes]* Don't worry Jamesy. My self-control is taking power. See what society has done to my moral conscience. I'm a moral coward. I'll never be anything else because I see things happening and I let them.

Jamesy What's come over you?

Toddy Sorry, old boy, I didn't mean it. Please forgive me and all that bull.

[Anxiously, Jamesy approaches him and facing him, puts a hand on his shoulder]

Jamesy Come on! Everything's all right now, isn't it? Between us, I mean.

[Toddy impulsively seizes James's hand]

Toddy Sure, it is! I got carried away. Even I'm entitled to lose control now and then.

Jamesy Of course! Of course! No man is made of iron. God, I'd be disappointed if you were short on temper. When I was five and you were six I thought you were the greatest fighter in the world. Do you remember?

Toddy Let's have something short. Did I hear you say there was gin in the fridge?

Jamesy You heard right, and there are lemons in the fridge and bottles of tonic water with the lemons in the fridge.

Toddy To hell with the lemons and the tonic water. Bring on the gin.

[Jamesy exits and returns immediately with gin]

Jamesy Do you think things will work out between me and the old man?

Toddy I don't know, Jamesy. He's a virtuous man. Always has been.

Jamesy Don't I know!

Toddy A funny thing…many people despise and ridicule a man of virtue. It's because they cannot be like him, I suppose.

Jamesy Some people are just weaker than others.

Toddy If a man doesn't measure up, his best reserve is ridicule. But never mind that now.

[He accepts bottle of gin and swallows from the bottle. Jamesy hands him a glass. Toddy pours and returns the bottle to Jamesy]

Toddy *I often think of home, dee-o-lea-day*
When I am all alone and far away
Bring me some ice, Jamesy, before I suffocate.

[Jamesy, anxious to do his bidding exits]

Toddy *[Lifts his glass]* Good luck, St. George and Harpy. God bless your innocent faces wherever you are. *[He swallows some of the gin]* God, I'm really beginning to feel sorry for myself. I wonder if it does any good feeling sorry for oneself.

[Enter Jamesy with container of ice]

Jamesy I thought I heard sounds of talk. Were you talking to yourself?

Toddy You heard sounds all right. I was humming. Believe me, Jamesy, people don't hum often enough.

Jamesy Terrible, isn't it?

Toddy It's a shagging disgrace, I tell you. Put some of that ice in here.

[Jamesy does so. Toddy drains his glass]

Toddy More gin, and don't be stingy.

Jamesy You're the boss.

[Jamesy pours two liberal dollops into both their glasses]

Toddy Now, you drink first. You're more expendable. You can't hum.

Jamesy *[He swallows]* I think we're on to something good here. It's intoxicatin', eh? Let's be serious for a minute.

Toddy But I thought we were being serious.

Jamesy Of course, but let's try to analyse our beloved father for a moment.

Toddy Alright. You begin. I'll examine your deductions and see what they're worth.

Jamesy Fair enough. Number one! He's domineering, too domineering by a long shot. He still wants to control us as if we were children. Number two, he's too

Goddam sanctimonious. Number three, his future is a major problem and number four, now I may be all wrong, but I have a suspicion that he's at the whiskey again.

Toddy Oh dear God no, you can't be serious.

Jamesy I hope I'm wrong, but I can't get rid of the nagging feeling that he's nibbling.

Toddy We had enough of that. You remember what he was like when he was at the whiskey before.

Jamesy I remember his best friends used to dodge around corners when they saw him coming.

Toddy Who're you telling. Many's the night I cried myself to sleep when he was on the rampage. We can thank Kate, boy. 'Twas Kate got him off it. You remember what that specialist said, another six weeks of constant drinking and your father's a dead man.

Jamesy We owe a lot to Kate. I don't know how she did it.

Toddy Now Kate is another problem.

Jamesy How do you mean.

Toddy Well, he's hardly going to live here alone, with her when we've all gone.

Jamesy Yes, it wouldn't work. You wouldn't consider taking him with you?

Toddy *[Laughs]* Not a hope. It wouldn't work. Anyway Penny wouldn't hear of it. What about you? You were always his little white headed boy.

Jamesy No hope. I've had enough lately. I don't want a lifetime of it. Look I love my father, but I have to think of myself.

Toddy Are you suggesting that I don't love him.

Jamesy No, I'm not, Toddy. All I'm saying is that he's a real problem and we'll have to do something.

Jamesy What can we do?

Toddy If only Ellie could be talked out of entering that Goddam convent.

Jamesy You can't do that.

Toddy He'll never survive on his own.

Jamesy He'll go back on the bottle.

Toddy That's what I mean and we can't have that.

Jamesy Maybe Kate would stay on.

Toddy Not Kate. Kate was always a great one for observing the decencies.

Jamesy Do you suppose there was ever anything between them.

Toddy   Not a hope. That's one thing you can be sure of.

Jamesy   If he sold this place and moved into a good hotel he could settle something on Kate. We all could.

Toddy   Hotels can be lonely.

Jamesy   What else is there?

Toddy   It's the best we can do for him I suppose.

Jamesy   We must think of what's best for him.

[He swallows and shakes his head at the impact. Enter Ellie and Penny dressed in bright summer dresses]

Toddy   Is this vision really mine? To be all mine one bright morning so very soon. You both look beautiful.

[Ellie hands Toddy his guitar]

Toddy   Oh, my old, my beloved guitar. Fifteen years old. There was respect for guitars fifteen years ago. Now everybody plays them, or tries to. What will it be, girls?

Jamesy Give us "*The Bold Fenian Men*".

[Both Jamesy and Toddy stamp their feet and come to mock-attention]

BOTH   *[Salute and sing]*
See who comes over the red-blossomed heather.
Green banners kissing the wild mountain air
Heads erect, eyes to front, stepping proudly together

Freedom sits throned in each proud spirit there ....

[Both march around the garden and come to a halt before the ladies. Ellie claps delightfully as does Penny]

Ellie More...More, please!

Toddy It's hardly an appropriate song for a beautiful summer's night. It's a night for bright songs, as bright as the summer dresses of these delightful women. We have it all-wine, women and song. I'm not sure about the song part of it.

Jamesy All right. What about "Genevieve'?

ALL *[Sing]*

> *Oh, Genevieve, I'd give the world to live again the lovely past*
> *The rose of youth is dew-impearl'd but now it withers in the blast.*
> *I see thy face in every dream; my waking thoughts are full of thee.*
> *Thy glance is like the starry beam that falls along the summer sea.*
> *Oh, Genevieve, sweet Genevieve, the days may come, the days may go,*
> *But still the hands of memory weave the blissful dreams of long ago.*

Toddy Ellie, give us *"The Black Hills of Dakota"* *[To Penny]* She's good at this.

Ellie *[Sings]*
*"Take me back to the Black Hills,
The Black Hills of Dakota…"*

[Before she concludes, JOSS enters and stands, with Kate, near the entrance, unseen by the others. Ellie leaps to her feet when she sees them].

Ellie Sit here, Kate, and you sit here Pops. *[She seats them both]*. Now to get the waders off…

[She succeeds in doing so and flings waders aside]

Kate I'd better get something to eat.

Ellie You'll do nothing of the kind. We had a huge supper. I threw everything I could into them.

Kate Then I'll get some sandwiches.

Ellie Oh, no, you don't. You stay right there near Dad.

Toddy Any luck with the fishing?

Joss Three fine sea-trout and lost as many more.

Penny Oh, I adore sea-trout. Where are they?

Joss Laid out lovingly on the kitchen table. But not for long, I hope.

Toddy *[To Penny]* You shall have sea-trout before the night is through. Fried sea-trout and we'll eat them out of our hands as if they were bananas.

Ellie   Now we'll have to have a song from Dad.

Joss   Aw, Goddammit, give me a chance Ellie. I've only just sat down.

Ellie   *[Mock-petulance]* For your little daughter, the nun, who's going away so soon. *[They laugh]*.

Joss   Well, will you listen to that! That's the roguery. They say that nuns are so good at wheedling that it's a pleasure to build them convents.

Ellie   Ah, please, Dad…Now, when did I last ask you to sing? My birthday, wasn't it? And where will I be on my next birthday? In a convent, with nobody to sing for me.

Joss   I think she'll be a Mother-General.

Ellie   A big hand, everybody. *[All clap]*.

Joss   Oh, all right! But not without ammunition. Penny pour me a beer.

Ellie   And Kate…Kate will have some gin.

Kate   Well…a little.

Joss   That's because I'm going to sing. She's not taking any chances…But what will I sing?

Ellie   *"Marguerite!"*

Joss   No bloody fear! The last time I sang that I nearly

Ellie   "*My Own Lovely Lee*"! Your favourite..

Joss   It was…a long, long time ago. *[Penny hands glass of gin to Kate and glass of beer to Joss]* Long life! *[He swallows all and coughs]*

Ellie   Attention, everybody, please! Jamesy, what's getting into you? There isn't a word out of you for the past ten minutes. Give him another drink Toddy. Now, Dad!

[Joss coughs again and commences song]

Joss   *[Singing]*
How oft do my thoughts in their fancy take flight
To the home of my childhood away
To the days when each patriot's vision seemed bright
Ere I dreamed that those joys would decay When my heart was as light as the wild winds that
blow

[All join in softly]
Down the Mardyke, through each elm tree
[All, strongly].

ALL

When we sported and played neath thy green leafy shade
On the banks of my own Lovely Lee.

[Applause]

Joss There, now! And the next time I sing, you'll see white blackbirds.

Ellie No, Dad...The next time you'll sing will be at your wedding...Now's the time to tell 'em... Listen, everybody...Daddy's got an important announcement to make...

[There is a brief silence]

Ellie Daddy! Don't tell me you're getting cold feet.

Joss I should think not! Why should I have cold feet... me of all people, with the most right. All right! You might as well know now as later. Kate and I are getting married. We haven't fixed a date yet but it will be pretty *soon* ...

Ellie Congratulations to you both! You have my blessing. Isn't it wonderful?

Joss What's the matter? Isn't anybody else going to congratulate me?

[The others exchange puzzled glances]

Toddy *[Laughs]* You can't be serious, Dad? *[Laughs nervously]* Some kind of a joke, is it?...I mean you and Kate...

Joss Why not? In fact, I'll tell you something else. If you and Penny have no objection, we'd like to have both weddings on the same day.

Joss *[Appalled]* What?

Joss Don't see why not. There's no law against it. You're the lawyer, Toddy. Is there a law against it?

Joss No, there isn't! *[Laughs nervously]* I just can't believe you're serious- We often joked about this and I hope that's what it is, another joke, with all due respects to Kate.

Ellie I'm surprised at you, Toddy. It's not a joke. Daddy is serious. He's made a very serious announcement.

Toddy He can't be serious.

Joss You mean, you don't approve?

Toddy I didn't say that!

Joss You didn't say it. But you don't approve.

Toddy It's a bit ridiculous, that's all. No, it's not ridiculous… But getting married -.. it's preposterous.

Joss I've got exactly the same right to marry as you have.

Toddy Oh, this is too much. Obviously you mean it.

Kate I'd better go in to the house.

Joss No! You stay right where you are! You'd better get used to the idea that this is where you belong.

Kate   No, Joss! I'm going in.

Joss   Very well. Go in. But it doesn't change anything.

Kate   Doesn't it? *[She rises, goes to exit, addresses all]* You can't get over it, can you? A lot more people of our age would be married if it wasn't for the narrowmindedness of their children.

[Exit Kate. A silence hangs for a moment].

Ellie   *[Downcast]* We really put our feet in it, Dad, didn't we?

Joss   I wouldn't worry about it, Ellie.

[Penny urges Toddy to talk]

Toddy   Since you seem to be serious, Dad, it's only fair to tell you that it would be impossible to have both weddings on the same day.

Joss   Don't let it worry you, Toddy. It doesn't worry me.

Toddy   You see, Penny's parents have made arrangements. The hotel is booked. The cards are being printed. Anyway, they'd want it to be her day and nobody else's. *[Pause]* You were married before. It's our turn now. We want the day to be ours alone. I think we have that right.

Joss   *[Claps]* Oh, my, that was beautifully said. I can see how a jury of juveniles would rise to that, or a jury of happily-married men, any sort of a jury so long as they weren't sixty-year-old widowers like me. You wouldn't impress them, I can tell you. You'd be laughed out of Court.

Toddy But I'm accepting it, Dad. I'm accepting it. I just can't understand the need, the necessity for it, that's all.

Joss And I hope you never will. *[Looks from Toddy to Penny]* I hope neither of you will and I really mean that. You talk about necessity. You young fool, what do you know about need or necessity. Do you expect me to rot? There is a need, boy; a crying, fearful need for companionship. Or do you visualise us making love…does it horrify you?

Toddy Please, Dad, not here!

Joss *[Laughs]* Lovemaking!…. What a beautiful expression! Maybe we will. Maybe we won't. All things are possible. I need companionship. You're not going to give me that nor is Jamesy or Ellie. You'll be gone, all of you, and I'll be alone. You take companionship for granted because you're young. I have to plot and plan for it carefully because I'm old and I could easily make a fool of myself. I'll accept anything but loneliness. Old men have so many worries about what lies ahead-they can't face it alone.

Ellie We understand, Daddy. You don't have to explain.

Joss None of you know this…but lately my hands shake a little and now I always manage to cut myself when I shave. I can't untie the knots in my fishing line any more and I can't tie flies or make minnows. I watch it when I go up the stairs. When I'm going for a walk or doing a bit of fishing I rest every so often. You see, I get pains in the chest and I know I have six or seven years, maybe ten if I watch it. If I go to bed early, eat the right things and stay off the liquor, maybe ten or even twelve, there's no telling, I'll might have as many as any of you. It's God's will.

Ellie Dad! You don't have to justify what you're going to do.

Joss No, Ellie, I'm not complaining about these things and I don't mind. Those are the handicaps of age and, believe me, I'm luckier than most. I don't mind *[Emphatically]* …but I do mind being alone and I'm taking timely steps to protect myself. Kate is my insurance against loneliness.

Toddy We understand, Dad. It's the suddenness.

[Ellie quickly comes between Toddy and Penny and takes an arm of each]

Ellie They're for you, Dad…What did I tell you?

Joss Ellie, you sweet kind soul. You see only the best.

Ellie Jamesy…*[She takes his arm]* But of course Jamesy is delighted. What's the matter with my Jamesy?

Jamesy Shag off, and leave me alone, will you?

Ellie *[Shocked]* Jamesy! You never spoke to me like that! All I asked is what you thought?

Jamesy All right. I'll tell you. I think it stinks. I think it's disgusting and unnatural. I've read about these things in the papers and I've laughed. The announcement is so sudden that it hasn't caught up with me yet. If you hear me laughing out loud in bed to-night, you'll know what the reason is…*[Laughs metallically and points at his father]* It's the thought of that sanctimonious old hypocrite getting married.

[Ellie retreats in shock]

Joss Why don't you tell her that you really don't care, that it's something else altogether that's troubling you… that you feel I'm to blame for stirring your conscience…that you're beginning to hate me because I want to turn you into a man.

Jamesy If you go on I'll never talk to you again. We're finished for ever. I'm warning you.

Joss You wouldn't change anyway. So what's the difference?

Ellie What have you done, Jamesy? What has he done… Toddy? Penny? What has he done, Dad? For God's sake will somebody tell me what's happening.

Joss He's getting married. But you know that, don't you, Ellie? What you don't know is that he has another girl in trouble.

Ellie *[Profoundly shocked]* Jamesy! It can't be true. Not our Jamesy…But Jamesy's so innocent…so good…say it's not true, Jamesy.

Jamesy I'm sorry you had to hear it, Ellie. It was a terrible thing to tell you, the most cruel and unnecessary thing he's ever done.

Ellie Oh, my God!…This is awful…awful…*[Hand over her mouth]* This is just awful. *[Tears herself away from Jamesy]*.

Jamesy Where are you going?

Ellie To my room. I'm going to my room. I'm going to pray for you. That's all we have left now.

Joss Come here, Ellie!

Ellie No, Daddy. I'm going to my room to pray for Jamesy, and for all of us.

[Exit Ellie]

Toddy This weather is getting everybody down. People don't really mean what they say *[Shakily]* It's the heat.

Jamesy It affects some people more than others.

Joss Silence please!

Jamesy Yessir!

Joss *[To Penny]* You knew about this, and yet you approve.

Penny It's none of my business. I never set eyes on Jamesy, or you or Ellie before yesterday. I'm not one of the family yet, so I have no opinion. I want Toddy and no matter what anybody's done I'm going to marry him. Jamesy was unlucky. He's done as much as anyone could for the girl, more than most would…Now he's getting married…He's going to settle down and I don't see how any of us have the right to criticise him…Take me to my room, Toddy, I've a headache.

Joss You don't really believe that what he's done should be treated as if nothing had ever happened. What about his responsibility to the girl?

Penny What about it? He didn't rape her. She could have walked away. There's an old groom who works for my father who puts it well…

Joss Oh!

Penny "If the filly is willing, she'll stand for it!"

[Exit Penny and Toddy]

Joss Why don't you go?

Jamesy Is that an order?

Joss No, it isn't. You should know that.

Jamesy Dad, I don't want it to be like this between us. What you did there with Ellie was unpardonable. She didn't have to know…but I'm prepared to overlook that because I know you're upset. You were never deliberately cruel-not even when you were drinking.

Joss It wasn't deliberate. But if we're to be friends again, Jamesy, you know what you must do. It's not the end of the world man. I've seen fellows like you who were shot-gunned into marriage and they're happy today. They've even got sons who're priests. *[Slaps his shoulder]* Wait 'till the kid is born…then you'll see. If 'tis a he, 'twill be called after me, of course. Let's have a drink on it.

Jamesy *[Draws away]* Goddammit, how stupid can you be? It's impossible. I'm marrying Marcella…

Joss Is there anything I can do to convince you?

Jamesy Give it up, Dad, and accept the inevitable. We'll have a double wedding, Marcella and I, and you and Kate

Joss So that's the bargain…Not a hope!

Jamesy In that case, you can go to blazes!

Joss A while ago you thought it was disgusting-Kate and

I—but now it's fine. What do you *really* think?

Jamesy Does it matter now?

Joss It does! Tell me, all other considerations aside, could you really approve of Kate and me? I'd like to know what you think.

Jamesy Well.. *[Pause]* …knowing your lofty principles and devotion to duty, I would approve, I would say yes…

Joss Do you mean that.

Jamesy Of course. There's a condition, however.

Joss Oh, what's that?

Jamesy Well, knowing your attitude to these matters, I would give it my blessing only if she were pregnant.

Joss You say this to me, your own father.

Jamesy You may be my father, but you're not my master.

[Exit Jamesy]

[END OF ACT TWO SCENE ONE]

ACT THREE

SCENE ONE

[JOSS sits in the garden, a bottle, a glass and a jug of water on the table in front of him. HE is in a concentrated mood of fairly advanced drunkenness. Solemnly he looks upwards, thoughtfully pursing his lips.]

Joss Oh, dear me, what a world; what a…goddam awful…bloody world.[*He pours from bottle into glass and solemnly adds water. Sips whiskey carefully].* Time I took proper stock of myself now. Can't seem to think clearly these days. I thought I knew my own sons. How foolish can a man get. Jamesy, Jamesy in particular. Jamesy was like my right hand and now the ungrateful hypocrites desert me, conspire against me. It's nice thanks after all my years, nice gratitude for the money and time I spent on them. *(Laughs bitterly)* Too old am I? I'll show them *(Shakes head and slaps table)* There's life in the old dog yet. By God there is. I'll show them who's commander-in-chief before this day is over.

[Enter Kate]

Kate *[Sternly]* Are you aware of the fact that you haven't eaten anything since breakfast?

Joss Yes, yes, I'm perfectly aware of it.

Kate   There's some stew on. You'd better come and have it.

Joss   No, thank you. No stew for me.

Kate   If you don't eat, you'll be sick.

Joss   Don't you think I'm old enough to know what I'm doing? Please understand that I don't want any stew. I'm having a quiet drink and I hope you won't take offence when I tell you that I don't want to be disturbed just now.

Kate   Look, Joss, my patience is stretched as far as it will go. I'm taking that bottle and you're coming into the house to eat something. You can't go on like this.

[She attempts to take bottle but Joss, surprisingly fast, seizes it firmly]

Kate   It's going to be me or the bottle, Joss. I'm warning you!

Joss   Now, don't be fussy, Kate. I have serious problems. I have to sort out this business of Jamesy and that unfortunate girl. For me, this is a time of crisis. I've been delivered a serious body blow and nobody knows how much it hurts.

Kate   And what about me? Where do I come in?

Joss   Patience, Kate! One thing at a time.

Kate   My patience is at an end, Joss.

Joss Ah, now, Kate! You must know the huddle I'm in.

Kate This is all the respect you show me, hitting the whiskey again after the promise you made me. You know what the doctors told you the last time. You won't last three months. Can't you remember that, you fool. You're digging your own grave every time you touch a drop of that poison.

Joss I respect you, Kate, but I will not have this sort of dictation from a woman who is to be my wife. I will not be called a fool. I'm sick to death of all of you. At every hands turn I'm baulked. My authority is being flouted in my own house…and now you join the pack.

Kate I'm for your good. You know that!

Joss I'll be the judge of what is good for me.

Kate You're not a young man any more, Joss. You must face up to it.

Joss It's not like that at all! My weakness is that I've been behaving like an *old* man. I've allowed myself to be treated like an old man. If people treat you like an old man, like all of you have been doing to me, it's easy to become old, to feel old. But I'm not old. By to-day's standards I'm young!

Kate Now I *know* you're a fool, when I hear you talk like this.

Joss   You don't like the truth, Kate. Is that it? You've called me a fool again, for the second time in five minutes. That kind of ridicule I will not take from anybody. Goddam you! What gives you the right to call me names?

Kate   I don't have to listen to your abuse, Mister. You're not going to treat me like a skivvy, Mr. High and Mighty. You've shown your true colours lately, Mr. Big Shot Retired Draper, with your grand notions.

Joss   Now, you're showing your true colours!

Kate   It's me that kept this house together when your wife died. I was sorry for you and the children and I came to look after you. You'd be growing daisies now, old man, only for me.

Joss   *[Violently]* Don't call me an old man!

Kate   This is nice thanks, isn't it-a nice reward for the long years I gave you.

Joss   God is the giver. Don't take credit for God's will.

Kate   I've enough of your drunken smut. I'm going home where something is thought of me, and don't you come running after me when you're in the rats. I have my own life to live. It's about time I started to look out for myself. No one cares any more about Kate Mulcahy in this damn menagerie.

Joss *[Rising]* Now, see here…

Kate You'd better see, Mister. It's time you cut out the preaching and had a long look at yourself. I know you for what you are. Who better knows you for the manky oul' man you are? Yes, manky, only I never gave you the chance.

Joss This is disgusting!

Kate It's about time, Joss you realised you're no different from any other old man who wants a woman.

Joss I'd have you know…!

Kate Oh, you'll get a woman alright. I don't deny that, but you'll have to come to your senses if you want a woman like Kate Mulcahy.

[Exit Kate]

Joss Merciful God! What's the world coming to?

[He rises, a little drunkenly, and looks after Kate. He swallows a little whiskey and goes drunkenly towards exit, bottle in hand].

Joss The fun is over now. By God it is! I'll show them who's boss in this house…Kate…come back here… I'm not finished with you…Kate!

[Exit Joss]

[END OF SCENE 1 OF ACT 3]

ACT THREE

SCENE TWO

[Action as before.
TIME: shortly afterwards. Night approaching.
JAMESY is seated at table, doing nothing and staring into space.]

[Enter Penny]

Penny Oh, I didn't know you were here! I didn't hear you come in.

Jamesy *[He rises]* I came in the back way. I thought it better to avoid the old man.

Penny He isn't in the house.

Jamesy Probably gone for a walk. It's been nothing but argue, argue, argue, these past few days. I haven't the stomach for any more.

Penny Have you heard the forecast?

Jamesy Forecast!

Penny The weather forecast?

Jamesy Oh, the weather forecast! What does it say?

Penny Heavy rain and thunderstorms moving in from the South-west.

Jamesy I'm glad to hear it. The fine days brought me no luck…When are you leaving?

Penny Any minute now. Toddy's gone to fill the car.

Jamesy Oh, he'll check everything. He always does. Oil and air and God knows what.

Penny He is painstaking, isn't he?

Jamesy It wasn't a particularly enjoyable week-end for you, Penny. You couldn't have come at a worse time. I suppose I should apologise to you but I feel you understand. There never was a week-end like it in this house.

Penny Your father is an obstinate man, too obstinate for his own good. He's riding for a fall.

Jamesy Oh, he's an upright man-or he thinks he is- but he's out of touch with the world.

Penny There's more to it than that. I mean, his wanting to get married again, at his age. It wouldn't be so bad if he picked somebody from his own class…were they living together, he and Kate?

Jamesy Living together?

Penny You know what I mean. Were they…?

Jamesy *[Laughs]* I doubt it very much. He's not that human! It just wouldn't occur to him.

Penny It wouldn't have to, if it occurred to Kate.

Jamesy Look, Penny, you could put Cleopatra into bed with my father and he'd leap out just in case he might do the wrong thing.

Penny Or the right thing!

Jamesy Most unlikely, believe me.

Penny He's well-off, isn't he?

Jamesy Yes, he's very well-off. He has a lot invested and he's still a director of the business.

Penny Then why doesn't he go out and get a woman and use a bit of commonsense?

Jamesy My father! Go out and get a woman! God Almighty, are you mad? I doubt if he'd know where to find one. He comes from a different school. He lives in a world where every man is a cavalier and every girl a virgin.

Penny There is no such world!

Jamesy There never was! Don't I know it.

Penny My father is different. He's broadminded. Of course he's a bit of a boy but he'd certainly understand your case. He'd laugh it off and give you a pat on the back. Tell you to be more careful in future. But he wouldn't take a very serious view of it.

Jamesy   I look forward to meeting him.

Penny   You will…at the wedding. Every six or seven months he goes away…on a *business trip*. About a year ago I saw him in a hotel in Dublin. I went up to see a sick friend. Her brother took me out to dinner. Just as we were leaving the hotel I saw my father. *He* didn't see me. He was booking into the hotel with another woman, a girl of my own age only she was prettier than I.

Jamesy   What did you do?

Penny   Nothing! The girl seemed genuinely fond of him and he of her.

Jamesy   You didn't tell your mother?

Penny   *[Astonished]* What good would it do if I did? He loves my mother…in his own way…but she's become careless. Besides, what she doesn't know won't trouble her.

Jamesy   Did you speak to him when you saw him with the girl?

Penny   You don't seem to understand, Jamesy. I respect and admire my father. He'd drop dead if I spoke to him… if he thought I'd found him out. He doesn't know I know and he never will and I love him as much as ever. That's all there's to it.

Jamesy   I wish my family were so broadminded. Does Toddy know about your father?

Penny   *[Laughs]* Toddy!…Toddy couldn't conceive of such a thing. I honestly don't think he could grasp it. That's why I love him.

Jamesy   He's a lucky man.

Penny   Thank you, Jamesy. I like you, too, and since you're the only broadminded in-law I have, it's important that we like each other.

Jamesy   Where's Ellie, by the way? Did she go out with my father?

Penny   No! She hasn't been downstairs all day. Kate took her meals up. I don't think she touched anything, though.

Jamesy   Is she sick?

Penny   I believe she complained of a headache. Kate doesn't tell me much. *[Laughs]*.

Jamesy   She resents you.

Penny   That's understandable. We come from different worlds. I don't mind. She's the one who minds.

Jamesy   She's shy.

Penny   No, it isn't shyness. It's ignorance, and ignorance is a wall you don't tear down overnight. Kate can never be happy. She'll always be afraid somebody won't accept her. I accept her for what she is, not an equal…because that would be hypocrisy…I think my husband-to-be is coming! Jamesy, don't worry. Things will work themselves out. They always do in the end, no matter how people behave in between.

Jamesy I hope you're right. It won't be my fault if they don't.

[Enter Toddy]

Toddy Are you all set? I'd like to be out of the city before the storm begins.

Penny I haven't said goodbye to your father or to Kate or to Ellie.

Toddy Hasn't she come down yet?

Jamesy Hasn't shown herself

Toddy The old man's just come in. He went into his study.

Jamesy Oh!…Oh!…

Toddy *[Explanatory*, to *Penny]* Always before a major announcement he goes into his study.

Jamesy And emerges with the most fantastic ideas.

Toddy *[Flatly]* He's been drinking.

Jamesy O, Suffering Son of God, no! Not again! Are you sure?

Toddy I'm sure. He was staggering. He also took a half-pint of whiskey from his pocket. He's a trifle incoherent, too, and his eyes are bloodshot. Satisfied....or do you want a blood test?

[Enter Kate wearing coat and hat]

Toddy Where are you going?

Kate I'm going to Blane.

Jamesy Anything wrong?

Kate *[Looks at Penny]* I'm just going to Blane.

Penny I'll run upstairs to say goodbye to Ellie.

Kate She's resting.

Penny Well, I can't go without saying goodbye..

Toddy Go ahead, Penny...but try not to be long. *[Exit Penny]...[To Kate]* But how do you expect to get to Blane at this hour? The buses have all gone, you know.

Kate I want one of you to drive me. It's the least you might do after the years I've given you.

[Toddy and Jamesy exchange puzzled glances]

Toddy *[Advances: Concerned]* What's the matter, Kate?

Kate I'm going home to my brother and I'm not coming back.

Jamesy No! You can't mean it!

Toddy You can't go! You're one of the family!

Kate I see no one inclined to welcome me into this family. You all got very cold when your father said he wanted to marry me, last night. You'd swear I was a common street-walker.

Toddy Marry him if you want to. Nobody objects, Kate.

Kate I don't see anyone jumping with joy.

Jamesy If you go now 'twill be the end of him. Who's going to look after him?

Kate *[To Jamesy]* You should have thought of that when you were acting the whoremaster.

Jamesy Now, see here, Kate….

[Toddy silences Jamesy]

Kate And that stuck up strap that's gone upstairs. She knows no better. Who is she anyway? All belong to me were honest people. I never wronged your father a penny all the years I was here. I worked morning, noon and night, except for the few hours I went home on Sunday…*[Starts to weep]* …nine long years and all forgot about in a few days.

Toddy You know what this will do to my father, don't you?

Kate   He's drinking. Isn't that it? Well, 'twasn't me started him off. I got him off it once but I'm not going to try again. I know the thanks I got.

Toddy   He's in no condition to drive you home now- probably wind up in a ditch.

Kate   I don't expect *him* to drive me.

Jamesy   *[Wearily]* Alright, I'll drive you home, if your mind is made up. Did you tell him?

Kate   I mentioned it to him this morning.

Toddy   What did he say?

Kate   He didn't seem to care one way or the other. I know my place. When you wanted me, I was the best in the world, but now that you're all fledged and ready to fly, I'm wanted no more.

Toddy   That's not true, Kate, and you know it.

Kate   It's true! If this was a night nine years ago, you'd be on your knees, all of you, begging me not to go. D'you remember, Jamesy, when I used to threaten to leave, you'd scream…and you, Toddy, used to turn as pale as a ghost and throw your arms around me, and there would be the two of you begging your own Kate not to leave you. *[Jamesy and Toddy look hang-dog]* … The monkeys in the Zoo have better memories… *(Cries)*….Well go on! Why don't the pair of you beg me now, throw the hands around the neck and say: "Don't Go!"...Mother of God, ye're a hard pair. I'm ashamed to say that I had a hand in the rearin' of you...I'll go out this way...Whenever you're ready, I'll be at the back gate.

Jamesy I'll be out when I see Penny and Toddy off. I won't be long. You can leave the bags. I'll bring them out.

[Kate suddenly runs to Toddy and puts her arms around him, then quickly exits. Exit Kate]

Jamesy I feel like a rat!

Toddy Now I know how Judas must have felt. We're a rare pair. When I look at you, I become ashamed of myself. But, then, you must have the same feeling when you look at me. Still, of the two of us, I feel sorrier for you.

Jamesy Don't be so righteous. It doesn't become you.

Toddy Oh, dry up!

Jamesy I would once, but not now. D'you know, it's a consolation to me to know that you're no better than I am.

Toddy Shut up, you fool! Here comes Penny!

[Enter Penny]

Toddy How is she?

Penny She'll be all right. Now, who's left… your father and Kate.

Jamesy Kate's at the end of the garden. She's leaving.

Penny Really! I hope it's not on account of me.

Jamesy It's not your fault. It's just the way things turned out.

Penny I won't say goodbye to her. She doesn't expect it from me, and I'm sure she'd only feel slighted by the way I did it.

Jamesy Here he comes! By God! He looks as if he'd solved the problems of the world.

Toddy Soused!

Jamesy He's plastered all right!

[Jamesy moves to other end of set. Enter Joss]

Joss *[To Penny]* I hurried back in case I'd miss saying goodbye to you.

Penny I wouldn't have gone without it.

Joss Good! Sit down! I think I may have the answer to all our problems. In fact I'm convinced I have. There is nothing that cannot be solved by reasonable men. Come on, sit down. *[They do so reluctantly]* Since I'm the senior member of this council, I'll take the chair, if there are no objections. *[All are seated]* You all know me. I'm a longheaded man, rather than a brilliant one. *[Laughs]* I'm not noted for my flashes of insight or brilliance. I built up my business from scratch. I built it the painful way, no dramatic takeovers or expansions, but tediously and carefully. But I got to the top from nowhere…that's what counts. Sit still, Jamesy! This concerns you most of all. I have reached this decision after detailed exploration of our problem and I have discovered a way out.

[Both boys are impatient]

Jamesy   Give us a cigarette, Toddy!

[Toddy does so]

Joss   I wish you wouldn't interrupt, Jamesy, and I wish you would show some appreciation for the fact that I'm still doing the thinking for this family. It is alleged that I am retired but when emergency arises there is nobody else in the house who faces facts as I do. No mean feat for a man in his sixties, eh? However… Name of God, Jamesy, stop wriggling or you'll try my patience. Toddy, you're the legal mind and yet the solution has evaded you. But I don't blame you. A man in love has other things on his mind.

Toddy   I wish you'll come to the point, Dad. I've fifty miles of driving to do and I want to be out of the city before the storm.

Jamesy And Kate is waiting for me at the end of the garden. I promised I'd run her out to Blane.

Joss It is I who am doing you the favour, gentlemen, and, since you are so impatient to be off…Be off! Be off at once! It doesn't matter a damn to me.

Toddy Sorry, Dad…Take your time…Go about it your own way. It's fine with me, if Penny doesn't mind.

Joss And Penny doesn't mind…Do you, Penny?

Penny Of course not.

Joss *[Viciously, to Jamesy]* God damn you, you young whelp, must you be so noisy, and don't think these grimaces you're making escape me. Pulling a crooked face is always contemptible when a man has the power of speech. Is there something you want to say?

Jamesy *[Sighs]* Sorry…I'll be like a block of wood!

Joss In all men there is a tendency to hide when danger threatens, but it's by facing up to things that great victories are achieved, as for instance Alexander against the Persians, although, if memory serves me correctly, he raped a kitchen slut in a moment of passion. Of course, in those days such behaviour was expected of Kings. The girl felt privileged for the rest of her life and I'm certain she boasted of it to her grandchildren.

Toddy Yes, Yes. I can well imagine….

Joss I can see her now with a host of smudgy-faced brats around her…yes, my children, the grandmother of your friends were sired by common men, but I…was mounted by Alexander. But values change…Where was I?

Toddy You said you were about to solve our problems.

Joss I did and I'll come quickly to the point, Toddy. You know this girl who fell foul of Jamesy?

[Toddy looks sympathetically at Jamesy]

Toddy Yes.

Joss And her parents…You've met them?

Toddy Yes, but I don't see….

Joss But if you're patient you will see. A little patience is all I ask.

Toddy Sorry, Dad.

Joss To-morrow I will avail of your professional experience. I'll pay you well. Double your fees, if necessary. Can I take it that you're willing to act as my solicitor?

Toddy What do you propose?

Joss You'll introduce me to this girl and to her parents.

Then I'll do the obvious, the one thing you all overlooked.

Toddy What would that be?

Joss I'll marry her. She will come here to live, to give birth to the child. She will remain until the child is reared. Then, as she pleases, she can go or stay. That's her concern. But my child stays, no matter what. Is that clear? The child stays with its father. I won't have my seed and breed scattered and trampled into the dust.

[Jamesy rises and takes Kate's bags near to exit]

Joss Sit down, Jamesy! I'll tell you when the meeting is over…or have *you* decided to marry her after all?

Jamesy *[Deliberately, slowly]* You dirty, drunken clown!

Joss I'll overlook that, since I no longer look upon you as my son.

Jamesy You're damn right, you will, because I'm getting out of this nuthouse. I've got a life to live and I want no drunken madman breathing down my neck while I'm at it. Sufferin' Son of God! Will you cop on to yourself?

Joss Say what you will, the decision is made. My duty is clear to me. What time do we leave tomorrow, Toddy?

Toddy Sorry, Dad, it won't work!

Joss Oh, yes, it will! You see, I'm not a man to shrink from my duty. This is not the way I want things to be. It's forced on me. I have to act in this fashion because there's no other course open to me. If you have a better solution, I'm willing to listen.

Jamesy For the love of God, Toddy, let's get out of here.

Toddy No, Jamesy, wait a minute. There's something you'd better know, Dad. The girl is gone.

Joss Gone!

Toddy She left for England this morning…to have the baby. Everything's been taken care of. She's happy, her parents are happy and Jamesy is free of all responsibility.

Joss *[Menace]* Oh! So they're all happy!….. *[He rises suddenly and slams table]* Well, I'm not happy; I'm not bloody well happy.

Toddy There's nothing you can do, Dad. The girl is gone. Jamesy gave me a cheque for £250 which I gave to her parents. They were damn glad to get it. Nobody will know she had a child and she leaves the home in London with no blemish on her character. She'll marry one of her own class after she comes out. They always do. The girls make excellent wives, have families and lead useful lives and, like I said, no one ever knows a thing.

Joss *[Who is rigid with fury]* Get up! *[Toddy rises, somewhat surprised and suddenly]* Come on! Get up! Get up! *[Toddy has risen]*.

Joss *[To Penny]* You, too!…Get up!

[Joss slaps Toddy across the face, Toddy is about to retaliate when Penny intervenes].

Joss What I need is a whip, or a stout blackthorn stick, to beat you out of here, the three of you, you Godless bunch of sorrowful wretches, you so-called Catholics! *[Laughs]* Catholics! *[Lunges at Jamesy, who avoids him easily]* You, that soiled your mother's womb and *[To Toddy]* you, the just man with the heart of a mouse. And *[To Penny]* you… My God! You take the cake…Get out of here and don't ever set foot here again, any one of you. I'm ashamed of you. While I live I never want to see any of you and when I'm dead, stay away. Stay away from this house, from my funeral and my grave!

[They stand shocked, rooted to the spot where they stand)

Joss *[Louder]* Didn't you hear me? I never want to see you again, any of you. You make me puke. Go on and get out. *[Shouts]* Out!…Out!…Out!…

Toddy Dad!…Dad!…Listen to me…

Joss *[Screams]* Get out of my house…You've disgraced me and your dead mother. Get out of my sight. *[Penny* *and Toddy exit hurriedly]*… out of my sight forever.

[Jamesy stands aside like a shadow unnoticed by Joss]

[Joss sits heavily on a chair and buries his head in his hands. Off-stage can be heard Ellie's voice calling]

Ellie *[Off]* Dad!… Dad!…What's happening, Dad?

[Joss does not answer but sits still, Ellie's voice calls again and again but he ignores it. He sits upright and shrugs himself into a position of dignity. He takes a half-pint of whiskey from his pocket and swallows some, but quickly returns it to his pocket as he hears Ellie approaching]

Ellie *[Off]* Dad!…Daddy!…Please!…What's happening?

[Enter a pale shocked Ellie, wearing a white dressing-gown held about her. First she hurries to exit and looks out]

Ellie So they're gone…is it for ever, Daddy, …is it? *[Joss does not reply, Ellie comes nearer]* I heard…and I can't say that I blame you…but it's not for ever?

Joss If you heard all, then you know all. It *is* forever. My mind is made up.

Ellie They'll come back. All of them. In God's own time. You've been drinking, Dad?…Say it's not true, Dad…please Daddy!

Joss Sorry, Ellie. You're the last person I would dream of hurting.

Ellie   We must fight it then.

Joss   They're all gone from me. I've no one now.

Ellie   You mustn't say that. I haven't gone from, you and I never will, Daddy…Never.

Joss   Oh, but you must…you must. You have a true vocation. You must go.

Ellie   No! My mind is made up. I'll stay here in this house, where I'm needed.

Joss   No…you mustn't…it wouldn't be fair to you.

Ellie   But this is where I want to be…Maybe this is where God wants me to be, where God's work is most needed. We must bring God back into this house. There's evil here. It's here now all round us. I can feel it. It's in the corners…It's everywhere. But it won't be here for long…we'll wash it away with our prayers, the two of us.

Joss   Yes, Ellie, yes. *[Wearily]* Yes! Yes! Yes!

Ellie   *[Puts a hand on the side of his face]* There is goodness and purity everywhere, Daddy…everywhere…but we must work for it…*[Withdraws her hand and touches her forehead]* Oh!…How beautiful…how wonderful…the first drop of rain. How I love the purity of the falling rain.

[She holds up her hands, palms upwards, while Joss locates his half-pint of whiskey]

Ellie   Oh! How marvellous! Here's more of it! One… two…three tiny drops. Oh, I hope it rains, and rains, and rains and the million of drops pour out of the heavens.

[JOSS produces the half-pint of whiskey and swallows some. He returns bottle to pocket].

Joss   Ellie!

Ellie   Yes, Daddy!

Joss   I have to go out for a little while. I won't be long. *[He rises somewhat clumsily but stands upright]*. Get your shoes on and some more clothes or you'll catch your death. There's a storm coming up.

Ellie   Where are you going, Dad?

Joss   Just out! I won't be long. I…promise. Now get your clothes on…Can I get you anything? Fruit or something?

Ellie   Don't go out! Stay here.

Joss   I told you I wouldn't be long.

Ellie   Let's say the Rosary. Let's say it out here in the garden. Who cares if the rain falls? We'll say it together.

Joss I have to go.

Ellie But the Rosary, Dad. You promised.

Joss Not now, child. Not now. My heart wouldn't be in it…I wouldn't mean it…*[Goes to Exit]* Now be sure you go indoors. I think we're in for a heavy fall. Yes, I think it's going to come down alright.

Ellie Daddy, I beseech you to stay with me a while. I don't think I can hold out any longer. I'm near breaking point. I'm not myself. I'm not well. If you leave me now, I don't know what I'll do.

[Joss is sympathetic].

Ellie Kneel here. Have you got a rosary?

Joss *[Searches]* It's here somewhere. *[He locates it].*

Ellie I know how you feel. You feel you must drink, but the grace of God is the answer.

[She puts Joss kneeling]

Ellie Now, Daddy, we'll pray!

[Ellie takes her rosary beads from the pocket of her dressing-gown and kisses the cross. Then she kneels on a chair and prays]

Ellie O' Sacred Heart of Jesus, look with pity upon this house. Have pity on my father and forgive the heartlessness of my brothers. Look with kindness into this garden, which is empty now and desolate. O, Sacred Heart of Love and Charity, let Your goodness, like the dropping rain, cleanse and purify us. O, Sweet Loving Jesus, I invoke Your Holy Name. Teach us to love each other so that our dead mother, who is in heaven, might receive us into her arms when we leave this place…

[Joss has risen and is about to exit]

Ellie Daddy! Where are you going?

Joss Don't persecute me, Ellie. I've had enough persecution lately.

Ellie But if you go out now, it will never be the same again.

Joss I wish you wouldn't addle me so much.

Ellie Dear God! What will I do with you. You're in no fit condition to go anywhere. *[She holds his arm]*.

Joss *[Petulantly]* Will you let go of my arm?

Ellie I won't…I can't I…I can't!

Jamesy He can't do this to me. He can't do this to me.

Joss *[Draws away roughly]* I know what's wrong with this house. I didn't rule with a firm enough hand. Well, that's all changed now! From this day forth…*[He staggers a little against table]* …there will be one law, my law, the law of Joss O'Brien.

Ellie   Oh, Daddy! You're hopelessly drunk!…Let me make some tea for you

Jamesy   No tea. Let him drink. Let the old fool drink himself to death.

Ellie   Please, Daddy! Please!

Joss   *[Shouts commandingly]* What's the matter with you? If you're to be a member of this household, these new laws apply to you. There is only one voice, one captain, one authority. Now, kneel if you want to, and pray if you want to, but…*[Emphatic]* …let me out of it!

[Ellie looks at him with pity]

Joss   *[Looks forward]* I'll rule with an iron hand from this night forward. *[Looks about him as if he expected a reply]* …Maybe I'll marry again…A young woman who'll give me children and this time…by God, this time, I'll make no mistake…*[Louder, with more emphasis. He lifts a clenched fist]* This time I'll rule with a mailed fist and I'll raise a God-fearing brood of Catholic Irishmen.

[His right hand stiffens as if he were about to suffer a stroke]

[THE END]

www.ingramcontent.com/pod-product-compliance
Lightning Source LLC
Chambersburg PA
CBHW070516100426
42743CB00010B/1837